The Power of Hype!

By **T.J. Rohleder**
(a.k.a. "The Blue Jeans Millionaire")

Other Great Titles from T.J. Rohleder:

Ruthless Marketing Secrets (Series)
The 2-Step Marketing Secret That Never Fails
Stealth Marketing
3 Steps to Instant Profit
Money Machine
Instant Cash Flow
The Blue Jeans Millionaire
How to Turn Your Kitchen or Spare Bedroom into a Cash Machine
The Black Book of Marketing Secrets (Series)
The Ultimate Wealth-Maker
Four Magical Secrets to Building a Fabulous Fortune
The Ruthless Marketing Attack
How to Get Super Rich in the Opportunity Market
$60,000.00 in 90 Days
How to Start Your Own Million Dollar Business
Fast Track to Riches
Five Secrets That Will Triple Your Profits
Ruthless Copywriting Strategies
25 Direct Mail Success Secrets That Can Make You Rich
Ruthless Marketing
24 Simple and Easy Ways to Get Rich Quick
How to Create a Hot Selling Internet Product in One Day
50 in 50
Secrets of the Blue Jeans Millionaire
Shortcut Secrets to Creating High-Profit Products
Foolproof Secrets of Sucessful Millionaires
How to Make Millions While Sitting on Your Ass
500 Ways to Get More People to Give You More Money

FIRST EDITION

ISBN 1-933356-85-5

TABLE OF CONTENTS

Introduction:

By T.J. Rohleder

"HYPE SELLS!"

Congratulations on your decision to read this book. After all, most businesspeople and entrepreneurs 'claim' they want to make more money, but how many are willing to pick up and study a book that can help them do it? I'm ashamed to say the answer is very few.

Yes, most people want the BIGGEST BENEFITS without paying the price to get them. You see this in all aspects of life, including business. And that's REALLY SAD because all the things you must do to get the BIGGEST BENEFITS in your business can be very fulfilling and even fun!

The secret? Just discover how to become A GREAT MARKETER. This is the key to dramatically increasing your sales and profits. It's the secret that gives you a MAJOR UNFAIR ADVANTAGE over all of your competitors... And once you get good at marketing your business, you'll discover that it is **THE GREATEST GAME ON EARTH!** Not only can this make you a lot of money, but it's also VERY REWARDING and a lot of fun!

Marketing is made up of all the things you do to ATTRACT and RETAIN the largest number of the very best buyers in your market. That's it. It sounds simple because it is! Of course, it's NOT EASY, especially in today's overcrowded and over-hyped marketplace. But tell me ANY GAME that's easy and I'll show you one boring game that you don't want to play!

The fact that marketing is difficult is **THE #1 REASON why none of your competitors will EVER get good at it.** Remember that. Think deeply about this and you'll see that **your ability to ATTRACT AND RETAIN the very best repeat buyers in your market is your key to making all the money you've ever wanted.** Sure, there's a learning curve you must get through. But that's THE PRICE you must pay to learn how to get good at ANYTHING you want to do. And I promise, when you get good at all of the things you have to do to MARKET YOUR BUSINESS, you'll have a major unfair advantage over all of the people and companies who are also going after the same prospects and customers you're trying to attract and retain.

So let this be YOUR #1 FOCUS as you go through this book. Have fun reading and thinking about all of the powerful ideas and strategies I'm about to share with you...

Here's What You'll Discover In This Book

This book gives you eighteen of my most powerful marketing secrets that I've used to generate millions of dollars in my own business. The first chapter is also the title of this book. It tells you **how to cash-in from THE POWER OF HYPE!** As you'll discover, this is an important marketing secret to getting the very best prospective buyers in your market to NOTICE YOU and your company above all the rest. You'll discover how the power of HYPE cuts through the clutter of all of the other advertising and marketing messages that your prospects and customers are subjected to each day. As I will prove to you, MANY OF YOUR COMPETITORS ARE SCARED TO DEATH to use this secret. They're so worried about offending anyone that NOBODY ever notices them! **I will go over this in detail in Chapter One.** I sincerely hope you'll use this secret to STAND OUT in your marketplace and get more of the very best repeat buyers in your market to do business with you! Please go over Chapter One to get these amazing secrets [which really are 'secrets' because very few or even NONE of your competitors are using them] and then enjoy the other marketing secrets I'll give you in the other chapters.

And to reward you for purchasing this book, I have...

A great FREE business-building gift for you!

Yes, I have a gift waiting for you that can DRAMATICALLY INCREASE YOUR SALES AND PROFITS! Here's what it's all about: I spent TEN FULL YEARS writing down all of the greatest marketing and success secrets I discovered during that time period. Each day, I took a few notes and, at the end of a decade, I had a GIANT LIST of 6,159 powerful secrets! This list is ALMOST 1,000 PAGES of hard core money-making ideas and strategies!** **Best of all, this massive collection is now YOURS ABSOLUTELY FREE!** Just go to: www.6159FreeSecrets.com and get it NOW! As you'll see, this complete collection of 6,159 of my greatest marketing and success secrets, far more valuable than those you can buy from others for $495 to $997, is absolutely **FREE.** No cost, no obligation.

Why am I giving away this GIANT COLLECTION of secrets, that took ONE DECADE to discover and compile, FOR FREE? That's simple: I believe many of the people who receive these 6,159 secrets in this huge 955 page PDF document will want to obtain some of our other books and audio programs and participate in our special COACHING PROGRAMS. However, you are NOT obligated to buy anything—now or ever.

I know you're serious about making more money or you wouldn't be reading this. So go to: www.6159FreeSecrets.com and get this complete collection of 6,159 of my greatest marketing and success secrets right now! **You'll get this GREAT FREE GIFT in the next few minutes, just for letting me add you to my Client mailing list,** and I'll stay in CLOSE TOUCH with you... and do all I can to help you make even more money with my proven marketing strategies and methods.

So with all this said, let's begin...

** WARNING: This complete collection of 6,159 marketing and success secrets contains MANY CONTROVERSIAL ideas and methods. Also, it was originally written for MY EYES ONLY and for a few VERY CLOSE FRIENDS. Therefore, the language is X-RATED in some places [I got VERY EXCITED when I wrote many of these ideas and used VERY FOUL LANGUAGE to get my ideas across!] so 'IF' you are EASILY OFFENDED or do NOT want to read anything OFFENSIVE, then please do both of us a favor and DO NOT go to my website and download this FREE gift. THANK YOU for your understanding.

CHAPTER ONE

We use hype and powerful promises for one reason:

To cut through the clutter of the thousands of advertising messages that are begging for our prospects and customers attention every single day.

◆ People are tuned out.

◆ They have created a tremendous resistance against ALL sales pitches.

◆ You have to do something dramatic to wake them up!

◆ You have to break through their zombie-like fog before you can pitch them.

The only way to do this is to be as dramatic as possible.

Use Hype and Powerful Promises

We use hype and powerful promises for one reason: because they cut through the clutter of the *thousands* of advertising messages that are begging for our prospects' attention every single day. You see, people are tuned out. They've created a resistance against all sales messages, so you have to do something dramatic to wake them up. **You have to break through their zombie-like fog before you can sell to them.** The only way to do this is to be as dramatic as possible.

Let's go back to our new wholesale printing club. **We've got a guarantee that's designed to do one thing and one thing only: blow people away.** Whatever the lowest price is that they can find on printing, our prices have to be lower than *that*, or we'll take the difference between the two bids and we'll cut the customer a check for double the difference. So if our lowest price is $1250 and they get it for $1000, we would send them a check for $500. What we're doing there is trying to just wake people up! We're trying to shake them up! We're trying to get them to say, "Whaaaat?"

There are so many marketing messages out there, and they're all so similar. Everybody's shouting. It's as if you walked in a room with a hundred people who all want to get your attention, and everybody's calling your name at the same time. Are you going to hear any one voice in that room? Probably not; a single voice is going to be drowned out. **Well,**

that's exactly how it is in the marketplace, so you've got to be different to be heard. You have to be bold. You have to be dramatic. Call it hype if you want, but it's got to cut through the clutter of all those other advertising messages.

Another big problem is that, because of the overcrowded marketplace, **people are skeptical.** They don't believe anything; they've heard it all, they've seen it all, and they're just not listening anymore. This comes in different levels, by the way: some people are mildly skeptical, while some people are totally cynical. They're beyond skepticism. No matter what idea you put to them, they're going to find ten things wrong with it.

You're doing yourself a disservice if you don't face up to that reality in the very beginning. You've got to realize that *this* is the person that you're trying to deal with. They're not going to pay attention. You're going to spend good money trying to reach them... and they're going to ignore you. I'm not trying to be negative here; I'm trying to be realistic. I'm trying to tell you what you must expect. **As long as you know that that's the way the game is played, then you can start mapping strategies out from day one so you can combat all that.** How do you cut through the clutter? How do you get people's attention? What do you have to say or do to wake people up, to get them to pay attention to you and what you're trying to sell instead of all these other things out there?

And that's another thing. People only have so much disposable income, so your goal must be for them to spend it on *you*. There are a lot of people trying to compete for that cash... **so you've got to be different just to wake people up.** You have to be bold and audacious like we're doing, as an example, with our wholesale printing club.

As a consumer, how do you choose who to listen to? There are all kinds of messages being presented to you. And on the flip side, **as a marketer, you have to do things to get your message across.** Chris Lakey and his wife teach an adoption class. They're in the middle of their fourth adoption as of this writing, and so they teach a class. They have this game they play, not only to introduce people to each other and new people in the class (it's an icebreaker type of thing), but also to get people to recognize that sometimes it's hard to figure out who to listen to.

So they hide an object in the room and blindfold somebody. They know that there's one person who is supposed to tell them where to go and direct them clearly... and everybody else is supposed to also tell them where to go, but they tell them wrong. So you've got all these voices talking to the person who's blindfolded, trying to tell them how to go find the object (usually it's a candy bar). Since everybody's talking, they don't know who to listen to. One person's telling them the truth; everybody else is telling them a lie... and they've got to try to figure out who's correct and who's not. What Chris is telling them is there are a lot of voices out there talking about adoption, so who do you listen to? **Who's giving you the correct information, and who's not?**

Getting your marketing message through the clutter of other messages can be a similar process. **People are bombarded with all kinds of sales messages, and they have to try to figure out who to listen to and who not to.** It all *sounds* good. You probably know, if you get business opportunity offers in the mail on a regular basis, that a lot of them sound good—so how do you figure out what's good and what's not? People are being exposed to all these sales messages, all these different offers, and they've got to figure out what to do. Well, most are just overwhelmed. They can't do anything, they get vapor-locked, and mail goes in the trash unopened because they can't think through it all. Therefore, as a marketer, you've got to find a way to get people to pay attention to you. **Give them a *reason* to pay attention to your sales message.** If you've got an envelope you're trying to get opened, give them a reason to open it instead of putting it in the trash. **To do that, you need to use hype and powerful promises to cut through all that clutter.**

Consider our guarantee with our new printing business. That guarantee is meant to break through the clutter and show people who are interested in printing that there's an incentive to pay attention. We're going to save you money, and we guarantee it in writing; if we don't, we'll give you double the difference back. **That message is meant to go over the top.** No printer is offering that guarantee; in fact, the best most can do is something like, "We'll guarantee we'll give you what you ordered. If you're not happy with the quality of our printing we might reprint the job. We're probably not going to give you any money back, though."

Well, not only are we guaranteeing the lowest price, but we're going to give you the difference back if you're able to find someone else who will do it for less. **That's a bold guarantee that's meant to cut through the clutter.** You can use something similar: double the money back if you're not happy, or you get a lower price, or whatever. A lot of stores do price matching; that's not really that big of a deal. **But we'll give you cash as a difference if we can't get you the lowest price.**

You can do it with an outrageous headline, too, a guarantee of something that people are going to experience when they do business with you. We use specifics with our headlines. Inside of saying, "You can make big money with our system," we might say, "Our system is actually a $1,000 a day system," where we put a specific number to it. It makes it sound more outrageous than just saying, "Our system will make you lots of money." **Using specific numbers that are a little bit unbelievable makes people want to find out what's up.** What's the catch; what's going on here? Do something dramatic to wake them up, breaking through the fog that is in their heads, the clutter they're experiencing.

They've got decisions to make. They've got to figure out how to prioritize what they're going to spend their time and money getting involved with. **You as a marketer have to find a way to be the one who breaks through.** Most people aren't creative enough to get their sales messages through. **So think like your customers;** think about them receiving your sales letter in the mail, think about them visiting your website. Whatever your sales message is, however you present it, think about your average customer and all the stuff they've got going on. Think about how easy it is for them to either drop your sales letter in the trash or click onto another website.

Think about those things from their standpoint, and then find ways to make them want to say, "I've got to stop and take a look at this." If you'll do that, your sales message will be read by more of your prospects, and you'll turn more of them into customers. And again, you can't worry about upsetting people too much. Here's an example: one of my latest books, a

600-page whopper, is titled "How to Make Millions Sitting on Your Ass." It's just a little controversial, that title. And when you read the introduction, you'll see it's all about sitting on your butt and working *on* your business, not *in* it (as I discussed in detail earlier). It's all about marketing, advertising, copywriting, that type of thing—things that you do while you're sitting on your butt behind a computer, preferably.

You can't be afraid of just going over the top just a little. Will some people be offended? Yes, of course they will. But you can't worry about that too much. **Worry about the people who aren't going to be offended.** When people are in a buying mode, they're in an emotional trance. Here's the best example that I can give: before my wife's MS got too bad, she used to want to go shopping a lot. We used to go to the Plaza all the time in Kansas City, and there was this Saks Fifth Avenue store that she wanted to go to. So I followed along and I had my book with me—I always had my book, and I'm the most patient person. As long as I've got a book, I'm like, "Take your time, Honey, take your time. No problem, I've got my book here." So I would sit in this store while she'd be walking around shopping, reading my book... but then, all of a sudden, I would notice how most of the women in the store were just in a fog, a daze.

I see this all the time. They were in the buying mode. **When people are in a buying mode, there's an emotional element that comes into play. And selling is an emotional thing; you want to pull people in.** You want to do things to try to be different than everybody else and get noticed. Realize just how bad a problem this is, okay? It's an overcrowded marketplace, where everybody shouts.

CHAPTER TWO

Direct-Response Marketing is a personal medium:

- Write and speak <u>to</u> <u>only</u> <u>one</u> <u>person</u>.

- The art is to make the person you are communicating with seem special.

- The more you can make them feel you are <u>only</u> <u>speaking</u> <u>to</u> <u>them</u> — the better.

W.I.F.M.

Strive to answer the question:

"What's in it for me?"

Radio Station WII-FM

Direct Response Marketing (DRM), which underlies just about everything we do here at M.O.R.E., Inc., **is an intensely personal medium.** What this means is that when you're writing copy, **you must write to only one person.** The art is to make the person you're communicating with seem singular and special (because they are). The more you can do to make them feel you're *only* speaking to them, the better. Why? **Because it all boils down to the principle known as WIIFM, which stands What's In It For Me?** WII-FM: that's the radio station everybody's in tune with most of the time, so if you really want to communicate with your customers, that's the radio station you'll need to broadcast from. **Any communication you attempt with your customers has to strive to answer that question: What's In It For Me?**

You can't expect them to figure it out all by themselves; you've got to be direct about it. **Tell them *exactly* what's in it for them.** It's all about salesmanship, which is a point I'm going to keep repeating. You'll probably get sick and tired of that, but the reason I have to repeat it is because in order to succeed, you have to internalize this, to understand it and appreciate it on an almost instinctual level. *It's all about salesmanship.* Think of the very best sales people that you know of. These people strive to speak *your* language, not theirs. It's not about what they want from you; **it's about what they can offer you.** That's their focus—and that's where your focus needs to be. Your communications have to radiate honesty and integrity. A kind of friendship is involved here. **You're striving to build relationships, to get personal with people.**

You'll see this focus everywhere when you study the best sales letters in DRM, the form of marketing that has made us more than $110 million. **DRM is simply salesmanship multiplied, through whatever medium you choose:** direct mail, Internet, radio, or TV. DRM does a great job of selling your prospects on the main benefit of your product, by making them a specific offer. **Ultimately, an offer is just all the things you're offering to give somebody in exchange for the money you're asking for.**

DRM is the also the only type of advertising that's 100% accountable—which means that you can monitor every dollar you spend. Almost invariably, you can tell what's working and what's not, because you're making people offers that ask them to take specific actions that can be tracked and monitored. That way, you always know where you stand. With other forms of advertising, you just throw it out there and keep throwing it out there, never really knowing if it's working. You're out of control. **With DRM, you have total control.**

But again, it *is* a personal medium, and it requires a high level of salesmanship, which must be based on an intimate awareness of the person you're trying to reach. Who are they? What are they about? What are they looking for? What do they *really* want? **That's why when you write a direct marketing sales piece, it needs to be written to a specific person, the person that your research tells you is typical of your**

marketplace. You want the reader to feel you're communicating only with them, so you say "you" a lot; you're trying to establish a relationship. You're not trying to make things too homogenized and bland. In a good direct marketing letter, there's a realness that goes along with this humanity that you're trying to get across.

And by the way: **don't be afraid to tell your new friend your story.** If I had to pick the one marketing strategy that's made us more money over the years than any other, it would be the fact that since Day One, we've been honestly telling our story. **We've been trying to get personal with people by telling them things about us that they can identify with, things that bond us together.** These are common experiences, things we know that they've experienced or may experience in relation to the kinds of products and services that we sell. That's part of the emotional element here.

We're getting involved in a new business right now that we really don't know a lot about... and yet what we *do* understand, and understand very well, is this principle of developing relationships with people, and having an intimate knowledge of who you're selling to so that you can communicate with them on a very personal level. **That way, you can make them feel special.** So while in some ways we feel like we're groping in a dark room looking for a light switch with this new business (which is a pet boutique, by the way) we're not letting that stop us. We're stepping out in faith; we're excited. We know how to excite other people about our products, too, so we're going to have a lot of different events, at least one a month. Now, these events might be very small, but we're going to bring people together to make them feel special. We're going to invite all our customers, knowing that very few will actually show. Even if they don't, they'll still feel special because they've been invited; and those who *do* show up will be treated extra-special. **Either way, we're doing this to get inside their heads and their hearts.**

We know that the ultimate success of our new business will be based on how well we get to know our target audience. Frankly, we already know them pretty well; but over time, we expect our understanding to grow, and we look forward to learning so much about them that our understanding becomes instinctual. To appeal to any group of people, you see, you've got to get behind their eyeballs. **A lot of this is just psychology and mathematics.** Over a period of time, we'll gain some intimate knowledge of who they are, and we'll be able to communicate with them in a much more impactful way.

All this may sound like common sense... and of course it is. **A *lot* of what you're going to hear from me is common sense, and yet most people in DRM just aren't putting it into action.** This is all very sad, because realizing that you're advertising to just one person, and then getting to know them intimately, is the foundation of any DRM campaign. You see people tripping over this concept constantly, just by using stilted language in their offers that makes it sound like they're talking to everyone at once. You can't appeal to everyone, and trying to do so is a mistake! **You've got to find *one* representative person and talk to them, like you'd talk to your best buddy on the phone.**

Some people argue that, hey, they have a product everyone

needs—for example, underwear or toilet paper. Okay, fine, maybe everyone *is* a prospect for toilet paper; that much is true. But that doesn't mean you need to make your appeal to everyone, because again, that simply doesn't work. With DRM, you have to make it sound like you're advertising to just one person. **You want to make it so that it feels like you're talking to *them alone* and no one else.**

The best way to sell something, of course, would be face-to-face. When you do that, you can get right in front of someone and make a case for why they need to buy your product, right there, right now. That's how door-to-door salesmen used to do it; even if you don't often see people selling vacuum cleaners and Fuller brushes that way anymore, it's still a great example. They knock on your door, you answer, and they give you a quick spiel—because you're probably getting ready to slam the door on them. **They know they've got seconds to make a first impression, to get you *not* to close the door at the very least.** If they can get past that initial resistance, they can make their sales presentation. So maybe you invite them into your house, and they spend however long it takes to make your sales presentation. They're hoping you ask some questions; and if all goes right, they end up walking away with a sale. They do that all day long, and get a lot of noes and a few yeses. If they're good enough at it, they make enough money to support themselves and their families. That's how you've got to approach this, especially if door-to-door just isn't your style. **And actually, direct response is better, because you can reach out and touch more people all at once.**

Let's say you're mailing a DRM piece to just one prospect.

THE POWER OF HYPE!

When they go to their mailbox, they pull out a bunch of stuff: bills, Publishers Clearing House sweepstakes, your letter and a few like it, and some sales papers. They take the mail into the house and starting going through it over the trash can, tossing the stuff they don't want and putting aside the stuff they think they should pay attention to. **Then they get to your envelope. Well, what do they do? You have a second, at the most, to make an impression.**

Let's face it: they're going to do one of two things. **They're either going to decide to trash your envelope because it's not important to them... or something will catch their eye that makes them hesitate.** There's something about your envelope. Maybe it's got some sales copy on it, or maybe they open it up and the headline on the sales letter catches their imagination and makes them want to read more, so they put it aside. Best-case scenario, they read it right then and there because it's just that exciting to them.

Your envelope is just like a face-to-face salesperson. **It has to get people to decide not to slam the door in its face — to decide to take the next step, and hear your entire sales pitch.** If you can do that much, maybe they look at your order form, and yes, they decide to place an order! That's how it happens in mail order. So when you're selling by mail, you want to speak to your prospect as if you were standing there in their doorway or at their kitchen table, trying to convince them to listen to you. **Your sales copy needs to offer them a benefit that speaks directly to them.**

Again, you achieve this by knowing your marketplace. **You have to communicate with them in a way that they'll**

understand. What benefits are they looking for? What's this new relationship going to do for them? **Once you determine that, sit down and write to them as if they're the only person reading your letter, based on what you know they want and need.** Since you can't go out there and deliver the sales message in person tens of thousands of times, you've got to do your best to personalize it. If you can, use their name in the letter. Instead of "Dear friend," or "Dear homeowner, " it's "Dear Jim," or "Dear Jane."

So the art here is to make the person you're communicating with seem special... which brings us back to their favorite radio station, WII-FM, where the only song that's ever playing is, "What's In It for Me?" That cuts through to the heart of things, doesn't it? People are busy. They've got lots of stuff going on, and they want to spend their money only on the things that are important to them, the items that, for one reason or another, provide them with what they consider true value. **So closely examine their WIIFM equation; and if you can solve if, you're well on your way to at least getting them to pay more attention to you than they would otherwise.**

Everybody wants to feel special, you see—and these days, the trend is to make people feel less special, especially where huge corporations are concerned. In his autobiography, *Made in America,* Sam Walton pointed out that to compete with Wal-Mart, all you have to do is offer great personal service. As he put it, the best he can do on that front is to have a greeter at the door saying "hello" to you as you walk in the store (and of course to keep people from stealing stuff on their way out). There's a severe lack of personal service nowadays, to the point where

25

you get put on hold for 20 minutes and there's this message that comes on every 10 seconds that goes, "Your business is important to us. Please hold." Obviously, they don't *really* care. People just don't feel that special anymore. **So when you go out of your way to make people feel that way, then you have a competitive advantage over everyone else in your market.**

CHAPTER THREE

❖ ❖ ❖

Use <u>plain</u> — <u>direct</u> — <u>simple</u> — and FORCEFUL writing that goes <u>straight</u> to the emotions of your reader.

❖ ❖ ❖

Be Direct

The way to make lots of money in this business is to use plain, direct, simple, and *forceful* **writing that goes straight to the emotions of your reader.** It has to be real, it has to be large, and it has to be human. You have to go right for the emotions. Now, what emotions am I talking about? **Well, the three big ones are pride, greed, and fear. You have to appeal to all three to make people feel special.**

This new business that we're starting is a pet boutique, with the ultimate intention of opening them coast to coast. Among other things, we're selling premium grade dog and cat food. **There are some terrible dangers of feeding your pet, things that they're not supposed to eat that's in all commercial pet foods sold in grocery stores.** People are mostly unaware of that, sadly. Well, all our pet food is going to be grain-free, because dogs and cats (cats in particularly) aren't made to eat grain. Companies put grain in their pet foods in order to boost their profitability, because it doesn't kill the pet... right away, anyway. But it *does* shorten their lives.

There are many health problems related to that type of diet, problems we need to educate our customers about that. So one of the headline ideas my marketing director, Chris Lakey, came up with was simply: "Are you killing your dog or cat?" **That's an ideal example of this concept of using plain, direct, simple**

and forceful writing that goes straight to the emotions. This example is designed to go straight for the fear factor by using short, punchy words: "Are you killing your dog or cat?"

This may seem like a rough way to get someone's attention, but it's necessary. People are busy; they don't have time to sit there and try to figure out what you're trying to say. **You've got a tiny window of opportunity to acquire their attention and get your message in there before they close the door on you.** You can't use big, complicated words; you've got to write in a way that a third-grader could understand. **Don't try to impress people; they're not going to be impressed.** They're going to be turned off, because they're just too busy to figure out anything complex. They want a quick headline idea, and when they hear someone ask, "Are you killing your dog or cat?," it's newsworthy. They're going to go, "Wait, what?"

Never forget that people are looking for instant results. I've already talked about radio station WII-FM. They want to know what's in it for them. They're selfish... and what's wrong with that? **We only have so much time, so we've *got* to be selfish and guard it.** Plus, they're skeptical and jaded; they're fighting to hold onto their money, so they don't trust people a lot. They're inundated with all kinds of ads and offers. There are all kinds of people trying to take their money... so you've got to do what you legitimately can to get to them. **If that means being blunt, so be it.**

Think of it as driving a wedge into a log; you can't split it until you manage to get the thin edge of that wedge into a crack. Once the wedge is in place, all it takes is a few hits from the big hammer to divide the wood... but it all starts with that small wedge. **Your marketing message is that small wedge, but to get it into a crack, you've got to slip past the typical consumer's shield.** That's hard to do these days, given all the competition. And just because you absolutely love your product or service, just because you're excited about it, doesn't mean that other people will be. That's another reason why you've got to be forceful. Try to find out your prospect's emotional hot buttons. Ask yourself: how can I use greed? How can I use fear? How can I use pride? How can I use a love? These are emotions that are already there, just under the surface. **Ideally, you've got to capture their attention by lassoing those emotions, so you can present the benefits of your products or service in a compelling way.**

As soon as Chris came up with the headline idea I mentioned above, I thought to myself, **"Oh my God, that's bold: "Are you killing your dog or cat?"** And then I thought, "Wait, is that a good long-term message for our store?" We thought about it, and figured out a way we could actually use a message like that and get away with it. That's going to be the title of a small information product we'll create for those who come into our store.

You *want* **to be bold. You want to be audacious, and you want your marketing message to be just a little dangerous.** Let me say that again: *you want your marketing message to be just a little dangerous.* If it doesn't scare you just a little, if you don't ask yourself, "Holy cow, can we really say that?", then you're probably not being aggressive enough. **You've got to think not so about much the people you're going to turn off as the ones that you're going to get through to.** They count a lot more.

So use short, punchy words. Become a student of good advertising copy. There's nobody better at it than direct response marketers, all of whom make their living on one thing and one thing only: **results.** As opposed to all this advertising written by people who've never sold anything in their whole lives. They don't know how to sell, even when they work for ad agencies and write ads daily. **When you're studying good direct response copy, you're studying people who *do* know how to sell.** They know how to get to the heart of the matter, to drive those wedges into the cracks of the skepticism and apathy that characterizes the marketplace—to command attention and make compelling arguments that cause people to get excited, to recognize that what's being offered to them is worth more than the money they're trying so hard to hold onto.

One of the things I think of when I consider this type of writing is the fact that you often see people trying to be creative in their selling process. They try to use humor, for example, and that's usually where they go wrong. Most of us think we're funnier than we really are, so when we try to be funny, we write sales copy that doesn't go to the heart of why we're writing. **Now, you *can* tell a good story; there's certainly a place for storytelling as part of your selling process, as long as the story relates to what you're selling, and to your ultimate goal of trying to get them to place an order with you.** But usually people just tell jokes, so their advertising isn't driving home the sales message.

This is easy to spot in TV commercials, because you see it all the time. There's a car dealership here Kansas that advertises on TV. For more than 10 years now they've used the same basic approach... and their commercials *are* funny. I always wonder how many cars they sell, because the owner tries to act like a comedian during his pitch. You see in that in a lot of TV commercials; they want you come into their store, and they hope that you watched their commercial because you wanted to laugh. Maybe there's some effectiveness there, or they wouldn't keep doing it... or at least, you'd hope not.

My recommendation is to avoid the funny. It rarely comes off the way you hope it will, and usually you get off-message. **Instead, use plain, direct and simple language that goes where you want it to.** Be forceful; be very specific about what you're trying to do. What's the purpose of your communication? Why are you talking at all? Going back to what we talked about on the last item: **tell them what's in it for them right up front.** Promise a big, bold, daring benefit to them to get them to read and respond to your offer. When you stray from the main reason why you're communicating with them, you end up costing yourself sales.

Take your subject straight to the heart of the prospect. Don't worry what others might think, because it doesn't matter who you upset—**it only matters who you** *sell.* Most people are too nice in their sales messages, too polite and politically correct, to get the point across. Well, when you're trying to sell to a certain marketplace, you have to know going in that you're not going to make everybody happy, as much as you might like to. It's just not going to happen, no matter how often you tell yourself otherwise. If you know that going in, if you can accept that *not* everybody will buy, then you can start asking yourself,

"What can I do to get the biggest percentage of the right kinds of people to buy?" **That's what lets you start to find the main benefits that your marketplace will respond to. Selling isn't about winning friends; it's about making sales.** If you offend or upset some people, that's okay. Now, if your numbers stink and you're not selling to anybody, there may be something else wrong there. But if your sales are good, it doesn't matter who does *not* respond, because some people won't. That's reality.

One of the great things about DRM is that you can make good money with bad numbers, as long as you make the offer to enough people. In some scenarios, you can have 95-99% of the people you mail your offer to say, "No," and you can *still* make good money. **It depends on the offer and the associated profit margins, you see.** Many factors go into that. But let's say 95% of the people who receive your offer don't like you at all. You can offend them, make them cranky, make them crabby. **It doesn't matter, because the 5% who responded are the customers you're looking for.** Now, I'm not saying to go out and *intentionally* offend people. You're not trying to stir up trouble. **But you do want to write to attract the people whom you want to respond, while not worrying about the rest.** You don't care much about what they think, so if what you say makes them not like you, in the end it doesn't even matter.

Stay on message. Stay focused on intently serving the people who will become your customers, by providing the most value and the biggest possible benefits to them. Just don't worry about the other people at all. Whatever they think or don't think about you is inconsequential, **because you're there to serve the customers who are going to buy**—the ones who are going to give you money. That's the point here. Use plain, direct, simple, and *forceful* writing that goes straight to the emotions of not only your reader at large, but specifically the people that are going to respond and become your best customers. And don't be afraid to tell a lot of stories, because stories help people remember you better. Just be real in every way.

CHAPTER FOUR

Work ON it — not IN it.

Be the architect of your business — <u>not</u> the worker or foreman. Definition: The architect designs the building — and sees to it that his plans are followed by the builders. The same is true in business. We must design successful marketing systems — and then monitor them closely.

Work ON It, Not IN It

This secret is something that a lot of people struggle with. I learned it from reading Michael Gerber's excellent book, *The E-Myth*. **In that book, Michael talks about the importance of working** *on* **your business, not** *in* **it.** You see, you've got to be the architect of your business, not the worker or the foreman. The architect is the person who designs the building; they see to it that the builders follow the plans. **The same is true in business: you've got to design successful marketing systems and then monitor those systems carefully.**

So look at your business as an investment, not a job. To do that, you've got to stay 100% focused on your marketing. **The marketing is the** *one* **thing you don't want to delegate.** And yet most people do delegate it, and even abdicate it... they just abandon it. That's a huge mistake. You have to keep the marketing for *yourself*. **And if you're not sure what marketing is, it's simply this: all of the things you do to attract and retain the largest percentage of the best buyers in your particular marketplace.** Whether it's a certain region or city, or the country, or the whole world that you generate most of your profits from, **your goal should be to stay 100% focused on that market,** attracting more customers and doing more business with the customers you currently have.

It bothers me to see business owners handling things that

any minimum wage employee could do... or even doing things that a person who makes twice that much could do. **Trying to wear all the hats is commendable, but not profitable.** It's such a waste of talent, but it happens constantly. I know smart people right now who are capable of doing work that can make them enormous sums of money, work that *has* made them enormous sums of money in the past—and yet they're spending a lot of their time doing things that will never bring them the big bucks. **At the very minimum, your goal should be to do one thing each day that has the potential to attract and retain more customers.** This gives you the potential to draw in thousands of dollars per hour —so don't let a day go by when you haven't done something substantial to bring in new customers, or do more business with existing customers. Think about that.

And think about the world's richest people. They have the same 168 hours per week that you have. They still have to sleep a fourth to a third of that time, and they've got other responsibilities and obligations that take up a significant part of their days. And yet they *still* manage to make hundreds of millions or *billions* of dollars a year. **Don't think that you're any different than those people! The only real difference is in their way of thinking.** For the most part, they focus on the most important things in their businesses, and hire other people to focus on the rest of it. **They really are working smarter, not just harder.** And sure, they're also working hard; believe me, it's a myth to think that the world's richest people are just a bunch of lazy, fat slobs. Don't buy into that. The world's richest people are working their asses off, too, but they're working smart. **They're focused on the most important aspects of**

their business, just as you should be.

Look, if you're an entrepreneurial type, then quit trying to manage your business. Entrepreneurs make terrible managers. **You've got to delegate all of your weaknesses to others.** Don't try to become stronger in the areas that you're weak in; **try to become stronger in the areas you're already strong in.** That lesson has taken me years to figure out, by the way! I once made the mistake of thinking that I could run our business. When my wife, Eileen, stepped down as President and CEO for health reasons a few years back, I stepped in, thinking I could do a better job than she did running the day-to-day business... and it just about killed me. Before that, I had no gray hair. Now it's everywhere. I almost lost some of my best people, because I didn't know how to manage people. I still don't know how to manage people. I can barely manage myself.

Entrepreneurs are dreamers, you see. If you want to be dramatic about it, they're visionary, creative types. They're the ones who think up stuff for other people to do. I think you need to spend a lot of your time just working in those areas. Where's your business headed? What are you trying to accomplish? You've got to try to see things three to six months away; that's about all. Forget the five-year business plan. **Have some long-term visions about where you might want to take the whole thing, but worry about the short-term first.**

I've told you about this pet boutique business we're starting now. We want to see these stores coast to coast. That's a long-term vision for us, but for right now our real focus is on trying to get the things right in front of us taken care of. Still, we're starting to talk about things that are going to take place nine

41

months from now. By talking about those things, we can start working towards them. It's just like when you're driving a car in the middle of the night, and you can see in front of you just a bit at a time. You've got to keep your eyes on that road and look a little bit ahead without overrunning your headlights. **That's also how you've got to keep your company moving forward.**

I want you to think deeply about the whole metaphor of being an architect, or even a general. The general is not on the front line; they're not out there shooting the enemy down. They have a good, overall concept of the whole war, the battle plan, and the strategies necessary to win that war. They're not focused on winning each and every little battle; they're focused on winning the war. You need to be like a general.

Every time I discuss this strategy, I immediately think of local service businesses, because it's easy to draw a contrast here between the way things are and the way things should be. Consider the local electrician or plumber—someone who started their business because they had a skill to market. There's certainly nothing wrong with that, **but what ends up happening is that they're unable to market that skill properly.** An electrician, for example, may be an expert at fixing bad wiring; and if you need a light installed or a switch wired in, he's your man. He spends all day doing that.

Well, usually the service businessman's idea of marketing is to run an ad in the Yellow Pages, and maybe he does a little word-of-mouth. He may very well end up with his schedule booked solid... **but he never really thinks beyond just doing the work. He's working in the business, not on it—every day,** Monday through Friday, and even some emergency stuff on the weekend. **Well, if he'd just stop and think for a bit about working** *on* **his business instead of** *in* **it, he might see an opportunity to expand beyond what he's able to do himself.** He's limited by the fact that he's just one person. Instead of doing all that work himself, he could hire a team of electricians who drive trucks around town, plastered with the company's name, phone number and website. He could build a team of people who work *in* the business, while he's in the office all day working *on* the business.

Maybe he likes doing electrical work, and he does some of it still... but he also has a secretary taking the phone calls and doing the scheduling, and he's managing a team of people who are out there doing the work. **That lets him spend more time thinking about all the ways he can advertise and bring in more revenue, and maybe expand the business even further.** When he's spending all day long doing the electrical work, they can't do any of that; he never has time to think much about their business in that way.

Working *on* **it, not** *in* **it, means spending more time thinking about ways you can make more money in your marketplace and serve your customers more.** I think that's where a lot of business owners go wrong. They spend a lot of time doing the work, but not really any time thinking creatively about their business. **You're the one who gets to dream about all the ways you can make more money serving your customers.** That's one of the joys of being your own boss. But when you're so busy providing your service, you don't have as much time to actually think about the ways that you can serve your marketplace and make more money with it.

 CŖƉ

Think in concepts.

See what others can't see — or overlook.

CŖƉ

Think in Concepts

To truly succeed in business, you have to think in concepts rather than isolated ideas. You've got to see what others *can't* see, or what they simply overlook. Now, the reason I chose to put this in is because most people *don't* think in concepts. **They think in details, and they get bogged down by them.** Whenever a new idea comes along, the very first thing they think about is, "How do I do it? How do I do it?" **Well, the how-to comes later, folks. First you've got to embrace the concept and put it into play!**

I've already mentioned our new business, and you'll hear me mention it again. At the moment, we're groping in the dark, frankly. We don't know much about running a pet boutique, but we're embracing the concept wholeheartedly, and we know that we'll find that metaphorical light switch eventually. Well, some of the people involved with us get locked into all these details: "How do we do this? How do we do that?" We don't worry about stuff like that! **We figure things out as we go. We stay focused on the concepts first.** This is a retail store that we plan to expand into a coast-to-coast chain... and it's starting out in Newton, Kansas, a town of 15,000 plus people. **Our goal is to put one of these in every town that size or bigger.** *That's a concept.* **We don't know how we're going to do it exactly, but we know we're going to try.**

Another concept that we're playing with is this: we're looking for about 500 customers to come in on a regular basis and spend $50-$100 a month. That's a concept. So how are we going to do it? Well, that comes later. **You figure things out as you go.** Your best ideas are never going to come in the beginning anyway. **By thinking in terms of concepts first, you** *then* **map out a plan that leads to the how.** You don't get bogged down by it from the get-go. We only have the vaguest ideas right now; that's the gospel truth. That's the way most businesses start out... and if other people tell you otherwise, they're probably lying. Nobody's got all the answers! **You have enough faith, enough confidence in yourself and the people that you surround yourself with, to keep moving forward, to keep finding solutions.** If you don't focus on the concept and you only start thinking about the details, you shoot yourself in the foot. You slow yourself down. You get locked into fear. You get confused and frustrated.

Of course, confusion and frustration is part of every business. That's why you have concepts. Whenever things get a little too overwhelming, you go back to the original idea you had in the beginning, the idea that was very conceptual in nature. When you're focused on the direction, you cross the bridges when you get to them, and you don't try to figure too much out too fast. **The plans are important, but your best ideas come as you move forward. And try to keep it simple!** As I told you, our ultimate goal for this little store that we're starting in Newton is to get 500 members. (We call them that because we're selling a membership program.) All we need is 500 members who come back on a regular basis and spend money. As long as we keep focused on that, we can work on the plans for how we're going to actually make that happen.

The more you focus on the concepts, the more the details will work themselves out. And things have a way of working themselves out as you move forward, too! Now, I know that all this sounds so generalized... but it really is that simple. Agonizing over the details right from the beginning is something that trips a lot of people up, especially analytical types and those who see in shade of black and white, with no room for gray. **They think that everything has to be figured out all at once, whenever an idea is birthed.** Even though it's just a baby idea, they start to tear it apart and tell you all the reasons why it's no good and can't work. That's counter-productive. **You need to wait on the negatives; let the idea become a little more mature before you tear it down.**

When you have a newborn baby, there's a certain way you treat it. You baby it, right? You talk to it in a certain way that protects the baby from the hard truths of life. As the baby starts getting older, you can come clean about those things. You don't tell the hard truth to a baby, or even a toddler or kindergartner or first-grader. If you go up to them and say, "Life sucks. You're going to work real hard all your life," the kid isn't going to be able to handle it. You need to shield them from the harsh things until they can survive them on their own... and that's the way you want to treat your baby ideas. Don't kill them before they have a chance to grow up a little. Now, maybe an idea *deserves* to be killed, eventually. **Maybe it'll never be a good idea. But you need to give it time so you can figure that out, and to let the little idea breathe.** When we have fresh ideas, or fresh concepts for some of our products or services, we'll often write up some general notes at the very beginning of the process and then let them sit for a while. We'll let the idea percolate a little bit in our heads. **So let the idea settle in a little bit; and then, later, you can start asking questions about whether something will or won't work.** There's plenty of time for that before you start really spending money on your idea.

This means that in the baby stages of the idea, you want to think in concepts. You want to ask yourself, "In a perfect world, what would things be like? What would this idea turn out to be?" The answers to these perfect-world questions are infinite, because no matter what the obstacles might be—if money were no object, if time and space were no object, if there were no hurdles to overcome... what could you do with this baby idea? **What would this look like if there were no obstacles? Dream a little.** That doesn't mean you won't have obstacles, it just means you don't worry about them in the beginning.

So, concepts first; details last. Let the ideas breathe a little before you squash them. **People who squash their ideas too soon end up never having good ideas, because here's the thing:** if all you ever work on are the very best ideas, or the ones that are obvious, you're going to miss out on a lot of opportunities that might have taken a little work to figure out. Sometimes, the very best things end up being the things you have to work a little bit at—where you think about what could happen in a perfect world, then say, "Well, I don't think I can do it that way... but maybe we could do it this way instead." **That's when you start figuring out ways to make it work instead of figuring out all the reasons it won't.** By thinking in concepts, you'll see past what other people are seeing. You'll see into areas they're not looking into. You'll explore opportunities they're not exploring... and you'll make more money than they're making. That's what I mean by thinking in concepts first and then figuring out the details later.

Keep the perfect world question in mind. Or do as another marketing genius that we've learned from does: ask yourself, "If I had godlike super powers and I could do anything I wanted, what would I do on this project?" **Stretch your thinking. Making money is a very creative process, and one of the best definitions for a genius is somebody who sees the same things that everybody else sees but sees them a bit differently.** People who are too detail-oriented end up hurting themselves, just by stopping themselves before they ever get good momentum going.

And one more thing when it comes to concepts: check your junk mail carefully. In fact, stop thinking of it as junk. **It's super valuable, because ideas are transferable.** Even if the mail has nothing to do with what you're selling, **the ideas may still be important...** as long as you get out of that detail-oriented mindset that keeps you from realizing the ideas are transferable. **Creativity is largely just stealing a little from a whole bunch of sources and putting it together in a unique way.** Recently, for example, we started developing an idea for a new wholesale printing club. Well, a lot of that idea came from another company we're involved with called My Harvest America. This company has a membership program offering discount groceries. And we thought, "Hmm, maybe we can do the same thing for printing." Basically, a lot of other things happened too; I'm not trying to say that only the one thing happened, but that was what we modeled our idea after. **We just figured out how to do it in another arena.**

We're also involved in another company called Global Domains International, and **part of their appeal is that it costs just $10 a month to get your own domain, email, website, the whole nine yards.** Everybody's got a ten dollar bill, so it's no big deal. So that's where we got *that* idea from. "Hmm, I wonder if we could put together a high-value service that saves people a lot of money and only charge $10 a month for it?" **You see, we're thinking in concepts. We're not getting bogged down.** To me, it's the most fun you can have. It's creative, and it's exciting.

CHAPTER SIX

Emergency money-making generator...

When times get hard...

When business gets slow...

When you need cash-flow to feed the monster...

<u>All</u> <u>you</u> <u>do</u> <u>is</u>:

a. Go to your best customers...

b. Make them an irresistible offer they can't refuse!

c. Have a special sale that will blow them away!

Do this and they'll stand in line with money in hand!

The Emergency Money Generator

When times get hard, when business gets slow, when you need cash flow to feed the monster, all you do is three things. This is another tried and true formula, and again, it's going to sound like common sense to you... but it's been worth millions of dollars to us. It could be worth millions of dollars to you, too. **Number 1: you go to your very best customers, people that you have a solid relationship with. Number 2: you make them an irresistible offer they can't refuse. Number 3, you have a special sale that will just blow them away.** If you do those three things, they'll stand in line with money in hand. It's simple; it's easy. You don't have to be very smart to figure it out; yet a lot of smart people *haven't* figured it out. That's the irony here.

Let's break it down in more detail. **First of all, your very best customers like you, trust you, and respect you. They already have a good relationship with you.** Because of that, they're always going to be open and receptive to new offers. **They have a buying history with you, so you know what they want in advance; and the more you know about your customers, the more you're able to create what we call "irresistible offers," which are simply offers that are just so good they just have to take advantage of them.** Take, for instance, this brand new company that Chris and I and a few of our friends are starting. We don't know anything about pet boutiques; it's in a whole different market area than anything we've ever been involved in. So one of the things we're going to do on a monthly basis is have special events where we invite our customers to come over for free. There's never going to be a cost associated with any of these events, and they're going to elements that bond the customers to us.

So it's part of our relationship building process. **But, here's what else it is: it's a way for us to get inside their heads and hearts.** It's a way for us to try to get to know them on a more intimate, emotional level. The more knowledge and awareness you have of the people you do business with, the greater your ability to attract other customers who are just like those people. That's how simple it is. **You cultivate your customer relationships, and when you need money, you go to your very best customers and just make them an offer that they can't refuse.** Why can't they refuse it? Because it's too good. It's value upon value upon value, and you just keep adding to it.

We've got a situation right now where we need to raise several hundred thousand dollars pretty quickly. If we were a publically-traded company, we would just sell some shares of stock and raise the money, just like that. But we can't do that. So what are we doing? We're going to our very best customers and making them an irresistible offer. We're giving them all kinds of great value, and that's how we're going to raise that money we need. It's so simple.

As the title says, this is an emergency money making generator, but it works well in a non-emergency situation, too. **When you absolutely have to make money, go to your best customers with an irresistible offer.** That's Marketing 101.

New customer acquisition is the most difficult thing you can do, because you're talking to people who don't know you, don't like you, and don't trust you—yet. You're making them an offer you *hope* they'll respond to. Usually, when you're doing lead generation, when you're trying to sell something to a first time customer, you're selling a low price-point item. You're just trying to get your foot in their door. You just want to make a great first impression and offer them something cheap, so they can raise their hand and say, "Yes, I want to try doing business with you. Hopefully, it will be a good relationship and we'll work together over the years, but right now I'm just making an initial small purchase." **Only then, after you've established that relationship, can you offer them something that's more expensive, or add them to the list of good customers that you want to establish long-term relationships with.**

So it's expensive and time consuming, and not always effective, to generate new customers. **Making money is much easier when you're doing it with people who know you and trust you—which is why we always say to go back to your preferred customers with special offers they can't refuse.** You see this done all the time across all industries. If you're on any mailing list or email list, you'll get special offers where they'll tell you they're having a sale. I've seen things where they'll say, "My wife says that I've got too much inventory. It's taking up the spare bedroom that she wants to use for crafting, so I need to get rid of it all. So right now, I'm making you a tremendous offer on everything in that spare bedroom. It's all 50 percent off. Here's a list, and here are the retail prices. Here's an order form, or you can go to this website to order."

THE POWER OF HYPE!

Now, stuff like that probably wouldn't work with a new customer; but it works just fine when there's already a good relationship established. **You know they're going to provide good value, so you want to respond.** You know that when you buy those products, you're going to get a good deal. That's what it means to go back to your best customers with an irresistible offer... and, yes, you have to determine what an irresistible offer is to your marketplace. **The offer you make depends on who your customers are, what they buy, the kinds of things they're interested in.** You should know all that because they're buying those things from you already. You know what they want the most.

We've done half-price sales where we tell our best customers, "Here's the price other clients are paying... but you can have it for half that." Now, it's important to have a reason why you're making that offer. If you just put something on sale, sure, you might get some orders. **But giving people a reason why gives them a reason to help you out.** It's all a part of the psychology; for people to do good unto you, sometimes they need an excuse. When there's a line at the store and a person just asks if they can cut, people almost always say "no." But if you add one word, everything changes. If the same person says, "Can I cut because... " the result will be completely different. What follows "because" isn't that significant, according to actual scientific studies.

This is what they tested: they had people ask, "Can I cut it to the front of the line because I'm in a real hurry?" and it worked, just because they said the word "because." The "because" got them off the hook, and people were more willing to let them cut. **So "because" offers the reason why. "I'm having this sale, I'm sending you this special invitation because..." whatever.** You have a reason for your sale, you have a reason you're making this offer. It could just be that you're trying to raise a little extra money. It could be that you're trying to clear some old product. It could be you're making way for the new model, the new inventory, and you want to close out all the last year's models. Your business will have a lot of possible reasons "why" that will apply. **Offering a reason "why" will help push people to respond, whereas they might not normally want to.**

To accomplish this, you have to segment your customer list—that is, separate out the better customers from the rest. Some people talk about the 80-20 rule, where 80% of your profit comes from 20% of your customers; for some companies, it's more like 90-10 or 95-5. Some companies are probably 70-30. **In any case, you need to know who your better customers are, and you do that by determining how much money they spend; that's usually the best indicator.** Strive to get to know your customers thoroughly: what they like and what they don't like, what they want and what they want more of. **That's the only power that marketers have, period.**

CHAPTER SEVEN

MASTERY

You do not become a MASTER by learning how to do 4,000 things... You become a MASTER by doing 12 important things 4,000 times!

Mastery

You don't become a master by learning how to do 4,000 different things. **You become a master by doing 12 important things 4,000 times.**

That's not just word play. There's a lot of wisdom in that statement.

Most entrepreneurs are unfocused. **They try to wear all the hats in their businesses, and by so doing, they limit themselves.** That may seem ironic, but you see, life is short. There's only so much time and energy available. **If you want to make the most money, you *have* to focus.** We have got a good friend, an absolutely brilliant guy, who could be making millions of dollars... and he should be. He's certainly made a lot of money in the past, but he has no focus whatsoever. He wants to wear all the hats.

Look, it's not about learning how to do 4,000 things that will make you money. **It's about focusing in on 12 things, or three things, or even two things. By doing them 4,000 times, you get good at them.** I believe wholeheartedly in this concept, because I believe in delegating all my weaknesses rather than trying to improve them. I'm only good at a couple of things, really, and that's about it. I've got other people who are strong in all of the areas that I'm weak in. For example: my wife ran the company for our first 14 years of our company. Eileen is really the businessperson, not me. I'm an entrepreneur, a marketer, a salesman. I helped with all the selling, the marketing, and the advertising while she ran things day-to-day. **It's all a matter of focus. Here's a good example to help you get the concept:** as I write this, it's a hot day outside. On a hot day like today, you can go out and get a good sunburn in an hour or so. That's about it. But if you take a magnifying glass and hold it for any length of time over a piece of paper, you can burn a hole in that paper. It's the same sunlight; but when it passes through the magnifying glass it's focused, and if focused enough, it can start a fire. If there's no piece of glass creating that focus, there's no fire.

I think that the one thing you should focus on, and never ever delegate completely, is your marketing. You have to get good at it. The more money you want to make, the more you should strive to develop your skills at marketing; or at least if you're working with other people, to try to understand the subject as much as you can. You see, a lot of people just abdicate their marketing; they turn it over to somebody else completely, and don't really want to know anything about it. **That's self-defeating, because that's the one part of your business you can't just blow off!**

And remember, when I say marketing, I'm talking about *everything* you do to both acquire and retain customers—all the steps you go through to initially attract them to you, and then get them to come back again and again. It's the one thing you should strive to know more about, because **it's one part of any business that actually makes money instead of just costing money. Almost everything within a business is an expense, except for two things: marketing and innovation.**

Innovation is anything that you can think of to improve your business, make it run more smoothly, and make it more productive—any new developments that you can imagine. I mentioned our new wholesale printing club earlier. Any time we spend tweaking that concept, fine tuning it, making it even better, working on ways to improve it, all fall under the innovation aspects of the business. **Like marketing, innovation is one of those things you need to master.**

So why don't business owners just buckle down and focus on these few important things? **I think it boils down to the fact that, again, they want to master everything.** They want to have their fingers in the pies relating to their businesses. Sadly, most people can't handle this. What ends up happening is that instead of doing one or two things really well, you do a bunch of things in a mediocre way. Let's say you're trying to keep the books, so you're working with the accountant on all the tax issues... and you're also taking orders and processing orders. You wear the shipping hat, the customer service hat, the tech support hat... and try to do all the selling as well.

So you end trying to do all these different tasks, and they all suffer—because you can only be pulled in so many different directions. **Instead of doing all those different things, if you would just focus on one thing, you could shine. That one thing should always be marketing.** There are probably 4,000 things you could learn about being a good marketer, but of course you don't need to worry about all of those when you're getting started. Even when focusing on one subject, some people want everything figured out before they ever begin; so they end up either getting overwhelmed and never getting started, or they learn just a little bit about a bunch of different things and don't have any depth of knowledge to help move them forward. Again: it's better to focus on just a few things and get those few things down really well, and then expand into other areas.

Chris Lakey is a political junkie; he studies the political news closely, and for the last few years has studied constitutional issues as an amateur, just by reading up on what our founders meant when they created the Constitution rather than what lawyers think about it today. He says that if he tried to learn all at once what he knows now, he'd be overwhelmed. But now he's knowledgeable and able to handle a lot of subjects due to what he has learned *gradually* over several years. **By learning slowly and absorbing things a bit at a time, he's got a good, well rounded understanding of many issues today.**

Here's an example of what you should focus on right away in your marketing, without worrying too much about the rest: **learning to write sales copy.** Make it a goal to learn everything you can about what it takes to write good copy. Sure, there are all kinds of things you can learn, but just work on sales copy for a while. **Become a master of what good sales copy looks like and how to write it, and then move on to something else.**

So: **spend your time, resources and energy on a small number of things instead of trying to tackle all of it.** I think that applies to your business in general. Instead of trying to do too many things and not doing any of them well, focus just on a few things until you master those, and then move on to something else. If that sounds like common sense, remember what Mark Twain said in the 1800s: **"Common sense is a very uncommon thing."** That was true back then, and it's even more true today.

◆ ◆ ◆

CHAPTER EIGHT

The best ideas are always an expansion and combination of previous ideas that worked.

◆ ◆ ◆

Rework Your Ideas

The best ideas are *always* an expansion and combination of previous ideas that have been proven to work. Now, in business, everybody wants to reinvent the wheel; everybody's looking for something that's totally new. **But the reality is that you don't have to reinvent the wheel, and you shouldn't.** I've told you that the idea for our new wholesale printing club initially came from a couple of primary sources; but there were some other sources too. We've got the initial concept laid out, but what we're going to be doing over the next few months is taking the best of the best of every single thing that we know has worked well in the past, and then adding to it.

It's just common sense. **Start with the best ideas that worked before.** If you don't have a track record, you have to study the marketplace. Get on the other side of the cash register. **Stop thinking like a consumer; start trying to think like a marketer.** Try to see what's behind all of this. When somebody is a consumer, their mindset is one way; when they stop thinking like a consumer and start looking around, watching what other people are doing, that's when it all changes for them. Look at your junk mail, for instance, and ask, "What's behind those ideas? Why are they doing what they're doing? Why are they saying *these* things, why are they doing *these* things?"

We're always looking for the best ideas we can find. **We're**

looking for those ideas that are going to generate millions of dollars, and *those ideas are already out there***.** You've got to believe it before you see it. There's an act of faith that's involved here. All of the money that you want to make—well, the ideas that will do it are out there right now. **You just have to find them, and lock into them, and figure out the right way to implement them. And it's always a combination of things that are working for other people.** Remember, ideas are transferable, so that an idea that's making a lot of money for one person can make a lot of money for you, too.

There's a saying that goes, "There's nothing new under the sun," and I believe it's from the Bible. Obviously, it was written thousands of years ago. Of course, some of the new inventions just in the last hundred years kind of challenge that quote; but think about it. Even the Internet is just another form of communication, and that's nothing new. Ideas are very similar to that. **Most of today's ideas are really just new takes on old ones—just fresh ways to look at things.** Jeff Bezos created Amazon.com because he thought that he could sell books on the Internet. Well, it's not that selling books was a new thing, because people have been selling books for a long time; it's just that Jeff thought there was a better way to sell them. In doing so, he created a really successful model. Now, of course, you can buy everything on Amazon.com.

The best ideas are just expansions and combinations of previous ideas. It's all about taking something you already know about and finding a better way to do it—like building a better mousetrap. **If an idea is too new, it can just cause you trouble.** There's a saying in our field that goes, "The pioneers get scalped." Those who try to tread new ground or invent something brand new usually struggle with that problem. The market requires a lot of education, sometimes, before they realize that there's a need for something.

Remember when the Segway came out about ten years ago? It was supposed to revolutionize city living and transportation; or at least, that's how it was built up before the big reveal. And what did it turn out to be? A gyroscopic scooter that goes maybe 10 miles per hour. Big deal. It's a little faster that walking. Mall cops and some police use them. But there was this huge hype before it appeared! It had a code name for a while, because they were keeping it under wraps. And then it came out... and everybody was like, "What *is* this thing? What do you do with it?" Well, they had to educate the marketplace on why you would even want such a thing, and what good would it do, and why they should pay $5,000 for it.

The Segway never became what it could have been, because they invented something brand new that was going into a new marketplace, and they had to educate people on it. They didn't do that very well, either. You could create a new car today and put it on the market, and people don't have to figure out what they can do with a car. They see a shiny new sports car, and they either like it or don't. But there's no educating them on what you do with a car, right? They don't have to figure out what to do with it.

New ideas just aren't like that. **That's my point here: that the best ideas of today are reinventions of other ideas. Many involve taking a couple of old ideas and merging them together into a new one,** like this new printing thing we're starting. Printing's been around forever, but we're coming up with a new way to do it where you can submit a project and get quotes back from printers all over the US, who fight for your business. It's a new take on an old idea, and that's what's important here.

So this method involves taking old ideas and coming up with new twists on them... reintroducing an old idea with a new angle, something that makes it new in the prospect's eyes. That's absolutely necessary. If I were to decide I wanted to sell mousetraps, I'm probably going to have to come up with a better mousetrap to get people to be interested in it, because you buy a mousetrap for what, a quarter? Fifty cents? They're very cheap, and they just do what they're supposed to do. So unless I come up with a better mousetrap, something that's brand new and creative and builds on that old idea, I'm probably going to have a hard time getting it into the marketplace.

So take old ideas, and come up with new angles, new twists, a new way to do things. **That's how you innovate these days.** There aren't really that many truly creative new things happening. Even if there were, most people won't appreciate you trying to "reinvent the wheel." People want a little something new, yes; but if you're going to do something completely new, you'd better have a history of past performance to show people... and look at what's worked best for you in the past. **Just keep trying to find ways of mixing things up so that they appear to be a little bit different even if, really, it's just the same stuff that's been working time after time. That's always the safest way to go.**

CHAPTER NINE

<u>Think</u> <u>on paper</u>!

The very act of putting your ideas on paper forces you to think!

Think on Paper

The very act of putting your ideas on paper forces you to think. I practice this constantly. Every morning, I get up before dawn and drink a lot of coffee while I write my ideas out on legal pads in longhand. I might have a whole stack of them in front of me, where I explore different ideas. **When you do this, you don't box yourself in; you try to look at *all* the possibilities.** You brainstorm a little. Play those things that I talked about earlier: "In a perfect world, here's what I could do," or, "If I had Godlike superpowers, and I could do anything I wanted, what would I do?"

Try to stretch your thinking, which is very easy if you do it paper. Have fun with it, make it a creative process, and practice considering all the different kinds of possibilities. I think most people would benefit from doing that. **Whenever you're confused or frustrated, grab some paper and just start writing and thinking it through.**

I may sound a little bit esoteric here, but here's something I think all of us might be able to agree on: there's what some people might call a higher side to all of us. **There's a wisdom when we tap into our creative sides where, if you just dream a little bit—or dream a lot—and think on paper, you can come upon some great insights.** You open yourself up to something special. It's part of the creative process. Again, part of creativity is combining all kinds of different ideas and trying to find new ways to hook those ideas together. You have to do it on paper. You can write all kinds of dumb stuff on paper, and nobody has to see it. You can throw it away, you can burn it, shred it, whatever.

There's just something significant about committing your words on paper, especially when you're processing ideas. **This is especially valuable when you're in the abstract stage, when you're thinking broadly.** Often, what happens is that you have a thousand ideas run through your head... but only a few hundred, or maybe only a few dozen, will actually stick in your brain long enough for you to remember them. In other words, if you try to just keep all your thoughts in your head, you'll lose most of them. So there's that aspect to consider... and of course, thinking on paper makes you think things through a little more in a linear fashion. **You're processing your thoughts as you write.**

Not everyone does it the same way, of course; in fact, not everyone uses traditional paper. Chris Lakey prefers to type his ideas into a Word file on a computer, because he types faster than he writes and his hand cramps easily. Once he's got a file full of notes, he can print them out and edit by hand. **The point is, whether you use paper or a computer, your thoughts become clearer as you work through the ideas this way.** You end up adding things you wouldn't have otherwise. A one-line idea can become a full paragraph just by fleshing it out a little, thinking it through, and adding some new touches here and there. **When it's on paper, you can keep a file full of all those ideas and refer back to them at will.**

In an earlier section, I discussed letting an idea sit for a few days to allow it to mature. Well, when it's on paper (or on electrons in a computer file!), you can let it sit there for as long as you like, then come back to it when you're fresh. **You'll see things differently, you'll have a fresh perspective on it, and you'll be able to add more and think things through a little more.** Thinking on paper is definitely better than thinking in your head alone. Get those ideas down in black and white!

If you're too busy to write something down or you think, "Man, that's going to be too difficult," then think into a voice recorder and have someone else write up the ideas. You can pick up a voice recorder at Radio Shack or online; they're not very expensive these days, and the cool thing is, they make them where you can record straight into MP3 or similar digital format so you can download the file directly into your computer if you want. **If you're driving down the road and you're thinking about a business idea, grab your voice recorder, turn it on and just start talking the idea out.** Even if it takes you an hour to drive, you're sitting there thinking ideas through, doing good work. Once it's on the recorder, you can find a local college or high school kid who wants to practice their typing, and they can transcribe your words so you can look at them later.

The point is, the act of thinking things through on paper or on audio helps clear your head a little; it helps you process what you're thinking, and lets you explore all the angles as they relate to what you're working on. And you should have fun with it while you explore, by the way. **A business *should* be fun. It should be a creative thing;** it doesn't have to be such a terrible, serious sort of deal. A lot of people treat it that way; in fact, we've got a guy we work with who's serious all the time, and who loves to find fault with everything before it's fully explored. He's very detail-oriented. We're starting a new business with him, and I'm always telling him, "Look, this should be fun." It shouldn't be a big headache. **This is the fun stage where we get to dream and think a little and air our dreams, letting our ideas grow.**

This new business that we're forming—that's how it got started. On January 15, 2010, I was going through my daily coffee-drinking brainstorming routine (caffeine helps to stimulate my thinking). I've got a building out on the property, where I was walking on this track. It's a long, narrow building; I was walking very quickly and I had a little tape player with me, and I started talking about this idea for this business. I just started laying some ideas down, and soon I had 50 minutes of audio. I had it transcribed, and we've continued to work with it ever since. The idea has evolved somewhat, needless to say, and we're going to have to constantly test new things, to see what ideas actually play out in the marketplace. **But we're having fun with it, because it *is* a creative process.**

Whenever you get confused, whenever you get frustrated, just start thinking on paper, writing things out. It's a great way to come up with new ideas, it's a great way to stimulate your thinking... and it's a *really* great way to tame some of that frustration you might have when you're confused about something.

CHAPTER TEN

Your intimate understanding of your market and core business is the #1 ingredient for riches.

The more you know about the customer...

a. What they have bought before — or are buying now.

b. Their problems, frustration, pain, hopes, and dreams.

c. And how your product — service — company can offer them a solution to "B" — the more effective you can be at selling them.

Knowing MORE about your customer lets you MAXIMIZE the up-sell.

The #1 Ingredient for Riches

How well you understand your marketplace and your core business is the number one determinant of how rich you'll become. The more you know about your customers — especially what they've bought from you before, or what they're buying from you right now, or buying from your most successful competitors — the better. **You also need to be vividly aware of their problems, their frustration, their pains, their hopes and their dreams, fears, failures, and frustrations.** The more you truly understand them at an intimate level, and how your product, service or company can offer them a solution to their biggest problems, the more effective you'll be in selling to them — and the more you'll maximize your profits.

Now, that sounds like common sense, and of course it is. But there are some very important things that I need to discuss as I break this one out, and **one of the most important things you need to understand is that *not everyone* is your customer.** That's crucial, because so many people don't get this point. They think everyone in the world is their customer... and so they target no one in particular. That's a huge mistake.

I've told you about our new pet boutique in Newton. Our goal is to franchise the business, to have stores in every city in the country. We want to sell *hundreds* of these pet boutiques. Most people have pets, and they love to treat them well. One of the key things we're trying to sell is premium pet food, and we'd like to get people to keep coming back repeatedly to buy it. We're starting in a town of about 15,000 people, so let's say that 40% of those people are pet owners; so now we've got about 7,000 prospective buyers.

But not *all* of those people can be our customers! Out of those 7,000, there may only be 1,000 or 2,000 who would come in and spend the money we want them to spend. Just because somebody owns a pet and *could* potentially come into our store and buy what we're selling doesn't mean that they *will*. And even if they come in once, it doesn't mean they're going to come in once a month, which is what we're looking for. Nobody's in business just to have somebody come in and do business with them once. **You're looking for people that you want to come back repeatedly.**

So you start with an understanding, as in this example; **an understanding that there are only so many prime prospects.** Most people don't realize that; they think anybody can be their customers. They don't have a clear enough idea of the type of person they're looking for. And sometimes, you can't really know who that person is until you do the advertising necessary to pre-qualify them. **In all cases, psychology is involved: you're sincerely trying to understand why they buy what it is that you're offering, what they're really looking for.** What are their problems? What are their hopes? What emotional elements cause them to habitually re-buy the kinds of things you sell? **Once you start getting a handle on that, you're looking for commonalities within your customer base, ways that you can communicate to them so it feels like you're speaking to them**

at a personal level. You need to resonate, so it feels like you're talking just to them. Part of this comes from getting to know them personally.

One of the reasons we do a lot of seminars and workshops with our parent company (we have 10-12 different events a year, on average) **is to stay close to the customers.** We want to understand them at an intimate level, so we spend some time with them, talk to them, get inside their heads and hearts. The whole time, we're treating them like royalty, doing our best to roll out the red carpet for them and give them the respect that they deserve. At the same time, we're like psychiatrists, trying to probe the depths of their psyches, trying to get behind their eyeballs, trying to think like they think. **And we're always asking ourselves, why? Why do they buy what they buy? What are they** *really* **looking for?**

One of the things you have to realize from the beginning is that **all selling is emotional.** While some of the questions we ask are logic-based, most of the answers we're looking for have more to do with emotions. Some niche markets are more emotional than others; for instance, this pet boutique. We're selling high-dollar items like expensive dog food. We're looking for people who have money and will spend it, because they're passionate about their pets. People who are passionate about their pets are, well, irrational. It's one of the reasons we chose this business model, by the way, because we're looking for a niche market with nice, rabid buyers. Rabid buyers keep buying and buying. Even in recessionary periods, they continue to spend money like crazy—and by the way, **the pet market is one of those almost recession-proof businesses. Number one, out**

of necessity: people have to feed their animals. But number two, because the emotional element causes certain people to spend a lot of money on their pets, no matter what.

With this new pet boutique, we're going to have our special events once a month. **One of the purposes of our events is to have our customers bond with us.** Even if most never attend, at least by inviting them, we'll create that feeling that we want to share with all of them. And, of course, we'll get inside the heads and hearts of those who *do* show up. We need to spend time with them, and the whole time we're friendly with them. We'll be asking them all kinds of questions... pointed questions, but ones that will hopefully go below their radar so they won't be able to tell what we're doing.

It all boils down to psychology. Just as a good psychiatrist probes their patient to try to get through to the core issues that brought that patient to them in the first place, **we're trying to ask probing questions to get people to open up. We're trying to listen carefully to what they're saying, but also to what they're *not* saying, in order to try to understand them at an emotional level.** That's where the power comes in. Our intimate knowledge of who we sell to has been the one secret that's made us millions of dollars over the past 22 years. So, if all this sounds simple to you, you're right. It *is* simple. The degree that you get inside the hearts and the heads of the people you do business with is the degree that you make money from them. **You have to understand them at an emotional level even more than they understand themselves...** because most rabid buyers don't know why they buy so much... because they're caught in the emotional aspect of it.

They can't possibly understand. They only have a small clue as to their behavior, much as a person going into a psychiatrist's office has only a small clue as to why they do the crazy things that brought them there to begin with. We're talking about the emotions here. So, there are parallels you can draw between a patient who goes to see a psychiatrist and a customer who comes to see you. Both are looking for something. They're both motivated by strong emotional forces that cause them to do what they do. **It's up to you to discover what those are, and then to develop more and more of what they want. That's the key to upselling them.**

Recently, Chris and I were having a conversation about this pet business. We spent a lot of time talking about this concept of getting in the minds of the customers and finding out what they want; and how, in the end, our desires for the business and the kinds of products and services we'll sell are only marginally important. **What's much more important is selling the customers what they tell us *they* want.** We both agreed that while we don't necessarily want to run the cash register, we would both like to spend some time behind the register just talking to customers—not because we don't have anybody else who could do it, but because of our deep desire, as part of the marketing side of our business, to know the customer intimately. That's what this strategy is really talking about. **It's an intimate understanding of the market, and who the customers are, that's ultimately important. It doesn't matter what your business is.**

If you're an absentee business owner, you're going to have a hard time figuring out what those customers want because you never talk to them, you never interact with them. On the flip side, with most local businesses, the person behind the cash register is the owner because they're a one-person operation. They don't have any employees. Maybe they've got someone part time who fills in a little bit here and there, but mostly it's all up to them. **If they're talking to customers all day long because they're the one behind the cash register, they're going to have a really good idea of what the customers want.** If a customer says, "I would like this brand of XYZ product," and you say, "Well, we don't have that," you might dismiss that as being, "Well, unfortunately we don't have this brand." But if people are coming in every day and asking for that brand, you should look at carrying it. You wouldn't know that unless you have an understanding of what your customers are looking for. Even if you're not in the store, hopefully you've got a manager running things who can relay that information to you.

So you, as the owner, need the input. **You need to know what your customers want the most.** This intimate understand of the marketplace is the number one secret ingredient to success, because your business is more than just the product you sell. It's more than your office or your storefront. It's more than the inventory on your shelves. It's more than your website. Those are just *things*. **The relationship is what is important.**

I envision an era day in American business history: Main Street America, the way it used to be, long before the digital revolution, before people started using computers to hide behind so they didn't have to actually talk to people anymore. You know, you don't ever see people send letters any more. I hardly know my neighbors. Chris Lakey is the same: he just moved, and as of this writing he's been in his house for about three months. His kids play with the neighbor kids, but their parents have yet to come over to introduce themselves and start a relationship with him of any kind. One of them did deliver a UPS package that was delivered to their house by mistake—and all she said was, "Hi. I'm your neighbor. Here's your UPS box."

My point is, people don't communicate personally anymore. But go back 50 or 100 years ago, and you had your Main Street gas station and your Main Street grocery store, and people went in all the time. They knew the owner, who thanked them for being in the store. There was a relationship there, developed over time. People didn't move as much as they do these days, so probably the grocery store owner was the same grocery store owner from when you were a kid until the time you retired. Since everybody stayed the same, the business owners knew their customers well. You went in and you said, "Hey, how's it going?" You talked about the weather or whatever and brought your stuff. **You *knew* them. There was a relationship there.**

To be successful in business, even if you don't know all your customers by name, you have to get to know what's in their DNA, what's in their make-up. What are the things they really want the most? **You have to acquire a deep understanding of who they are, even if you don't know all of them by name.** In our business, we've worked with hundreds of thousands of people. There's no way we could know all of our customers by name. And yet, we have a few that we *do* know by name, because they come to our events. We know them because they've been here, or they've come and taken a tour of our offices. If we were to see them at Wal-Mart, we would say, "Hey! Howya doing?"

We don't have that relationship with all our clients, because most of them we never hear from. They buy something from us by mail and maybe they've never contacted us for support, and so we have no personal interaction with them. But aggregately, for the sum total of our clients, **we know what things they're interested in, and we know that by studying what they're buying from other companies and what they're buying from us.** We know their buying patterns. We know the kinds of products and services they're looking for, because we're constantly looking at that information.

So, whether you have a storefront, whether you do business by mail or on the Internet, **you've got to do things to build relationships with your clients, and to have that knowledge of the general marketplace you serve...** What kinds of things they respond to, what kinds of offers they're looking for, what products and services they want, what pain they're in, what problems they have that you can help solve for profit. That's part of your goal in business. So rather than focusing on what your product is, what your service is, start by focusing on your marketplace.

What have they bought already before, or what are they buying right now? **Focus on their problems, their frustrations, their pains, their hopes, their dreams, their goals, what they're looking to get out of life, what challenges they face, and then use that information to figure out how your company can offer them an alternate solution.** Their universe is on a track for destruction. They're in pain. They've got some sort of a challenge or problem, and if things don't go differently somehow, they're going continue down that path. So offer them a Plan B—an alternate ending to their story.

And you can frame it like that in your marketing. It's like they're standing in a fork in the road. They've received your advertisement by mail, on the Internet, or in person. **Now they've got a choice to make: Choice A,** to continue down the path they're on and get the same results, continue to be in pain, continue to experience that same old suffering — or **Choice B,** to take the fork in the road and try your solution. You've got a product that alleviates their pain, maybe literally if you're in the medical field and you've got a supplement that will help them feel better. Maybe their pain is that they're struggling with obesity—and you've got a solution that alleviates their pain. Just days from now, they could be feeling better! But they have to choose the right path.

And maybe they're not *exactly* **in pain. Maybe you're just offering them more of what they already have.** Consider the types of products we offer to businesses. Maybe the business owner is already doing fine... but we can help take their business to the next level. So we're not really solving pain as much as giving them the ability to increase their revenue and do even better than they already are. **Whatever the choice is, you're looking at a stark contrast between what they have as their status quo and what they want to ultimately achieve.** If they don't want to stay the same, then they have to go down a different path. Your product or service, your solution, should offer them a better way.

The way you determine what that is is by understanding

what they're looking for. **You've got to understand their problem in depth before you can offer a solution.** The more you understand your specific marketplace, the more effective your problems will be. Knowing more about your customers lets you make the most money by providing products, services, and solutions to them—again, common sense. Yet some people are taking it to a whole deeper level than others. **They go beyond the surface and start digging deeper, because they know that that's where the power is.** That's where you begin to understand your customers better than they understand themselves, and can speak to them more effectively. **If you use DRM, you can speak to large numbers of them at once.** You could have thousands of clients, and you could be speaking to them in a way that really connects them to you, and makes them want to keep coming back and doing more business with you, which is ultimately what you're really trying to achieve.

CHAPTER ELEVEN

5 Elements Of Every Super-Successful Direct-Response Message:

1. Meaningful specifics — <u>not</u> vague generalities.

2. A promise.

3. An offer or offers.

4. Precise commands — *"Here's what I want you to do now."*

5. An extra reason to act immediately.

— Dan Kennedy

The Five Elements of Every Super-Successful Direct Response Message

This next secret comes from my friend, Dan Kennedy, a brilliant marketer from whom I've learned a lot. **Dan says that there five elements of every super-successful DRM message:**

1. **Meaningful specifics, not vague generalities.** Be very specific in all of your copy, in all the words that you use.

2. **A promise.** I would amend that to say a bold, audacious promise.

3. **An offer.**

4. **Precise commands.** For example, "Here's what I want you to do right now." You're telling people exactly what you want them to do.

5. **An extra reason to act immediately.** Something that will go away; something that's available only for a limited time.

Let me start off this topic by saying that all DRM is salesmanship. For a direct mail package, it's a sales presentation in an envelope; if it's online, it's a sales presentation on a website. But it's salesmanship either way. Part of what salesmanship is all about is performance; that's one of my definitions for selling. I use to say that selling is serving, and

THE POWER OF HYPE!

I still agree with that somewhat. Selling *is* serving, but serving has no real power. **It's more about giving people the performance, giving them what they truly want, delivered in a way that none of your competitors are doing.**

As part of that performance, you're very focused on what they want. Think about salesmanship. This is not advertising; this is not marketing. It's salesmanship, and think of all the good qualities that a salesman has. Think of someone you know who's a dynamic salesperson. Just focus on them for awhile; spend some time thinking on paper a little, and writing down all the qualities that make that person so great at selling. Part of it is that they make you feel understood. **They make you feel that you're special.** You're not just a walking wallet to them; that is, it's not just your money that they're after. A good salesman never gives you the idea that all they want is your business. **It's all about what they can do for you.** That's part of what Dan is talking about here with the promise. You're very specific about it, but it's a promise.

Back in the 1700s, there was a gentleman named Dr. Samuel Johnson who said that the promise is the soul of the advertisement. That's even truer now than it was three hundred years ago. **When you look at good salesmen, you think of people who are very bold.** They put it all on the line. They're very audacious in many ways. They can be loud and proud sometimes, and then sometimes they can be very quiet. **They can be the world's best listeners.** They can be your best friends. But they're *always* making bold promises—like our promise for our wholesale printing club, where we promise that we're going to save people 23-76%. Not 24-77%, but 23-76%. We're not just going to save them money, we're going to save them 23-76%. We're very specific here. **Be clear about that promise, whatever it may be, because vagueness will hurt you.**

We recently wrote an amazing sales letter for our wholesale printing club. It's only two pages long, and yet it's just a $10-a-month service. But then we realized, "Hey! There's no offer in this." So immediately we added an offer. **An offer is simply all the things you're going to do in exchange for the money you're asking for;** but very specifically, it usually includes some bonuses you're going to throw in, or some special deals you're going to make. In this case, it's a $10 monthly service, but for $99 they can join for a whole year. So they get to save money, and they don't get their credit card whacked every month. Now we've added four more bonuses; if they just take the $10-a-month plan, they can choose one of any four bonuses. **We spell out all the bonuses on a separate sheet, make it very attractive, using colorful images.** That's part of the whole presentation. If they take the $99 deal, we'll give them all four bonuses. That's part of our offer, too.

Remember, we don't really sell products and services: we sell offers. Everybody wants a special deal, and our job is to give them what they want. So you've always got to think about that: the customer wants a bargain. **They want to feel like you're going to give them something that's just for them, so you've got to make them a special offer.** That offer could be saving money; it could be some guarantee; it can be all the free bonuses that you're going to offer. It can be a limited time sort of thing: today only, or this week only. It can be a reduced quantity, or something else — **but there always has to be**

something. It's not just, "I've got this product, and if you want it, come buy it." That's a terrible sales pitch. You've got to give people a reason to act now. **You've got to incentivize them.** They expect it, all good DRM gives people incentives to act right now. It makes them specific offers, and the promise has to be bold.

Once you've got a promise in place, and you've made the offer clearly, you've got to tell them exactly what to do. You've got to make this very clear. You can't pussyfoot around or be vague. You have to tell them exactly what to do: fill out the order form. Fax or mail it to us, or give us a call today. **Be very, very clear. You've got to put them under some pressure, too.** They have to respond by a certain date, or there's a limited time offer, or something like that.

Right now we're producing a package that's going to go out to all these business owners. I told my graphic artist, "I don't want this thing to look too corporate." I get a lot of business mail, and it's all too neat. It's too clean. It's too pretty. It's too homogenized. It's too *perfect*. The language is too careful. It's been produced with this great care, and yet it all just looks phony... and it's easy to ignore. If there's an offer in there, it doesn't shout it loud enough. So I told my artist, "Look. This thing can't be too corporate. It can't be too homogenized."

So one of the things that she did was that take that promise we made in the pitch and blow it up on the envelope. If you're a business person and you're busy and you've got all these solicitations, if you're being pitched by all these different people who want your money and you're separating out the mail over your trash can like all businesses do, it's going to hit you very, very hard. **That big, bold statement, that promise that we're making, is just going to nail you between the eyes.**

Then you go through the pieces. The way we've used our color and laid it all out, I don't want to say it's dirty, because it's anything but. Yet there's an element in there where... well, let's just say it's got a lot of salesmanship to it, okay? **There's a lot of selling being done in the direct mail package, and it's produced by people who have an eye towards selling.** So much of the advertising these days is done by people who have never sold anything in their lives! They don't know how to sell. They *can't* sell. They even have bad attitudes about salesmen; they never want to think of being a salesman.

You've got to get rid of that mindset completely. You've got to be proud to be a salesperson. Selling is what we all do— *everybody*. Sometimes I think we like to call ourselves marketers just to avoid that reality. But come on! **We're all salespeople, and DRM is salesmanship.** It's *all* salesmanship. So study great salespeople. Study great sales pitches, so that when you hear one you can recognize it. **Learn the difference between good and bad by keeping your eyes open and getting on the other side of the cash register.** Start saving the good ads, the good sales letters, when you see them. Model your ads, your websites, and all of your communications accordingly.

The idea here is to keep it simple, and I think that even though there are a lot of complicated formulas in this field, this is fairly easy to do. Sometimes you see people with long checklists for things that need to be included in every direct response message. Well, this is just a foundation. Of course, there are many things you can put in an offer, **but these are the basic things you want to make *sure* are in there. Get these all in, and then worry about the other elements; with these in place, you've got the foundation for a successful sales piece.**

Again, start with meaningful specifics, not vague generalities. This is one of the things we see people flubbing all the time. Here in the money-making field, that usually means someone claiming that their new money making system has the potential to make the user "a lot of money." Well, that's all fine and dandy; everybody wants to make a lot of money. But a vague headline like that isn't going to pull as well as a headline that says: "Make a $1,000 a day," or, "Make $12,642 a month." **Specifics are always better than generalities when it comes to income claims, or mathematical examples, or anything like that.** Now, the caveat here is that **you have to be truthful**; don't make things up. If you've got a specific, income example, you always want to use it. That's much better.

People respond to them more readily, and they're more believable. If you just say, "this offer can make you millions," well, what does that mean? It's a vague generality. It's better to say, "This has the potential to make you X dollars," where you inject a specific number. **That number becomes credible, just because it's not vague.** Meaningful specifics *always* trump vague generalities.

Next, the promise: what are you going to do for them? Think about how you can fulfill the needs and wants of your prospects. **Think about them receiving the benefits you're offering, and how that will make them feel.** If you're selling a

98

health product, your promise is going to be some health benefit; an alleviation of pain, for example. **If you're selling moneymaking opportunities, your promise should be about the results that they're going to achieve when they buy your opportunity.** To determine the promise, you have to practice the last principle: intimately understanding your marketplace.

You want to make a bold promise: some big guarantee or statement based on your knowledge of who your average customer is. This is something we want to do in our new printing business. I've talked a bit about our promise of having the lowest prices on printing—a guaranteed, bold promise. You're never going to find printing that's cheaper than ours, and we're backing that up in writing, with a guarantee that pays the customer double the difference than if they actually *do* get a printing job done somewhere for less. That's a bold promise for people who buy printing services. We're saying, "We're going to guarantee you prices lower than you can get anywhere else, so don't bother looking."

Some people will see that and take us up on it. Some people will see it and say, "Ah, hooey. I *know* I can find printing cheaper. I'm going to go to my local printer. I know he always gives the best deal, so I'm going to take your bid and he'll beat it." That's great. We *want* people to do that. We're confident that our prices are going to be the lowest—that through our printing network, we're going to have the ability to get better prices than most people are ever going to find on their own. But if you can beat us, so be it; we welcome the challenge! Still, most people aren't even going to bother trying to check us on that. They'll see the claim and take it at face value. **They'll feel like they're**

getting a good deal just because we tell them we have a guarantee. That bold promise is something that'll make people decide to do business with us who might not otherwise.

So you want to make some kind of outrageous statement—but make sure it's true, because you don't want people to check you on it and find out you're lying. If you do have a big promise you can truthfully make, some outrageous guarantee or claim, make it boldly. Be proud about it. Some people will check you on it, and they'll find that you're telling the truth. Others will just believe that it's the way it is because you say it is, and they won't bother checking. **It'll help increase your sales, because it will help people feel better about doing business with you.** I often think about fast food restaurants making claims that they have the best burger. According to whom? Well, it's mostly opinion, but they throw a claim out there, and people believe that *must* mean they have good burgers. Making an outrageous claim about your product or service is definitely something that will help you get more sales.

The third element: an offer. Sometimes you get so excited talking about your benefits that you don't really go through all the elements on the list of basics—and so you forget the offer like we did with our little newsletter recently. Mistake! **You always want to make sure you have an offer in there.** Now, you do want to give them a reason to respond immediately (per element number five), but that's essentially an extra reason— maybe a P.S. or some other reason to act now. A main offer is a reason to come into the store. Maybe it's buy one get one free, or take 25% off the whole purchase. Maybe it's a bunch of free bonus gifts.

The fourth element is the command—telling them what you want them to do. You'd be surprised how much people like being led; it's one reason you see countries succumb to Communism and other unworkable political philosophies. People *like* being controlled... and if you don't like that, well, I'm sorry. That's the way life is. Most folks like to be told what to do... and certainly, when it comes to personal freedom we don't like that as a culture. It's not a good thing, but in business it's something you need to be aware of. You simply need to tell people exactly what you want them to do. **Tell them *precisely* how you want them to respond to your offer.** If you want them to fold up the order form, stick it in an envelope and mail it to you, tell them to do that. **If you'd rather they pick up the phone and call, tell them to Call Now—and give them your phone number multiple times. If you'd rather them fax your order, tell them that.**

Whatever you want them to do, just *tell* them. If you have a local store and want them to come in and buy, tell them to cut out the coupon attached below and bring it in between now and next Saturday. The sale ends at midnight, so don't be late! Don't miss out! Print this coupon off, bring it in, pick out all your merchandise, bring it up to the front, hand it to the clerk—and you'll instantly get 25% off your purchase! **Tell them precisely what you want them to do, because if you don't, they'll be left *wondering* what to do.** There will be some confusion. **You'll miss orders because you weren't direct and obvious.**

And then the fifth element: give them that extra reason to act immediately. You have your main offer; you've done a good job of presenting the specifics. You've made a promise to them. You told them what you want them to do, so now give them an extra incentive to act right now. This is like those late-night infomercials on TV. The offer is this: you buy this set of knives, and you're going to get everything you see here for two easy payments of only $19.95. *But wait, there's more!* Because we want you to act right now, we're going to give you *twice* as many knives. Now you can have a set to give away for Christmas. Just pay the extra shipping and handling, and we'll double the order!

This little extra bit is designed to push people over the edge. Sure, you know people are interested in what you have to offer, so you're going to get a certain amount of orders as long as you target your market properly, and as long as you've got a good product. But that extra incentive to act *now* will push more people over the edge. **You've got fence-sitters waiting, wondering if they should take the time to order.** People have stuff going on in their lives. They're busy. That extra incentive, an extra reason to act immediately, makes them go, "Oh, gosh, I can't miss out on that! I need to take action now. I don't want to put this offer down, because I know I'm inclined not to come back to it again."

Whatever that action you just told them to take, give them a P.S. Give them an extra reason to do it. "By the way, while you're looking at this, I want to let you know that if you order before midnight tonight, we've got this super double bonus. You're going to get this, and this, and this. If you wait till tomorrow, that's not available." Or, "By the way, for the first ten people who call now, we're going to throw in this and this." It's just a little extra to push people over the edge. They're already thinking about buying. This extra reason to act immediately pushes more of them over the edge.

You may think, "Well, my offer's good. I'm getting a good response right now." **Yes, and if you don't have an extra incentive, you're probably missing out on business that could and should be yours.** Maybe your response rate is 10% right now. That's phenomenal! People are buying and it's crazy busy… but you just don't have that extra reason to act immediately. Maybe that one thing could boost the response rate to 15-20%. **You don't have to give them a price cut; just add more value.** Tack on more bonuses to make people want to say yes. Unless the sales model you're using is strange, you'll probably have enough profit margin there that any bump in response is going to pay for the cost of whatever bonus you gave away, or whatever extra incentive you provided.

And you might find that instead of just bumping your response rate a little, the extra thing is what tips you over the edge from marginal profitability to a huge success. **So always do a little more. Always give people an extra incentive to do business with you.** Make your offer, work on your sales piece, work on your website, whatever your method is—make it a good offer, and then go back to the drawing board and say, "What else can I do to make people jump over the edge? What else can I do to give them an extra reason to act today?" Then implement whatever you come up with. **That extra element can really have an impact on your bottom line.**

$ $ $ $ $

CHAPTER TWELVE

Customers in all markets want someone to do <u>everything</u> for them.

$ $ $ $ $

You must sell people the things they want — <u>NOT</u> the things you want to sell them!

* It's all about them, not you.

$ $ $ $ $

It's All About Them, Not You

You have to sell people *the things they want*, **not necessarily the things you think they need, or the things that you want to sell them.** You have to go all out to give them just what they want, the way they want it; and more and more, they want more and more. **The trend these days is for customers in every market to want someone to do** *everything* **for them.** People are just so busy, you see. All of this technology that was supposed to make our lives so much easier just makes it all the more complicated. People are overwhelmed.

Also, the consumer is spoiled rotten. You've heard the old saying: *The customer is king*. Well, not any more. **Today's customer is more like a dictator — and a child dictator, in many ways.** One of the smartest marketers that I know says that from an emotional standpoint, we're all little children in adult bodies. I like that. Children want everything, and they want it right now. You have to protect them from that tendency, because they'll eat candy all day long if you let them. Well, from an emotional standpoint, consumers are like little children. **They want to be waited on, they want to be catered to, they love to be spoiled, and they want superior service.** A lot of them are lazy, quite frankly, and they're getting worse.

But then again, capitalism is based on giving people what they want. **So ask yourself how you can do more for your**

customers. For instance, this little pet boutique that we're getting ready to start: one of the things we're going to implement within the first six months is a delivery service. Pet food is heavy; asking people to get in their car, drive over to your store, and then lug around those bags is asking a lot for some people. So we're actually going to deliver their pet food to them. A wild and crazy idea, maybe... yet restaurants are doing it all the time nowadays. Grocery stores are starting to deliver groceries again, like they used to in the old days. You've got the rent-a-car places that will come pick you up now. Netflix will deliver movies to your door so you don't have to walk into a Blockbuster store.

People like to be waited on. The more you can do to treat them like the little kid royalty they want to be treated like, the better. And that really *is* how it is. Now, this is not about making judgment calls on people. People have more choices than ever before; that's one of the great things about Capitalism. To give you a fast, maybe a slightly absurd example, my wife wanted some Oreo cookies a couple of weeks ago. So, on a Saturday night I trekked over to a tiny grocery store nearby, and I found about five different kinds of Oreos. It used to be that they had just the one kind, then they had the double-stuffed too, and now they've got mint and white vanilla Oreo cookies... and there were two or three other kinds, too. **Today the average consumer has more choices, and companies are catering to those choices, and you've got to do the same thing for your customers.** Give them more, more, more of what they want the most.

That starts with finding out what it is that they want the

most of, and why. Earlier, I talked about being a psychiatrist. You need to get inside their heads and hearts, probe those "emotional waters," and really try to figure them out. Also, spy on your competition! The Internet is great for legal corporate espionage. Incidentally, you can also go visit your competitors' brick-and-mortar locations. We've got a local competitor for our pet boutique, and I've gone in that store half-dozen times to snoop around—trying to figure out what they're doing right and what they're doing wrong. Chris Lakey told me about another competitor, and we're going to adopt some of the things they're doing. **So you get ideas from studying what other companies are doing, both your direct competitors and, if you're really creative, your indirect competitors.** In fact, you'll find yourself stealing ideas from all kinds of sources. That's fun; that's the fun part of business.

Look, who ever said that business has to be completely serious? Business can be fun: it's challenging, it's creative, it's rewarding, it's stimulating, and, certainly, **when you want to make the cash register ring, you really do have to cater to people.** By the way, I went and met one of our competitors a couple of weeks ago. I drove to Kansas City and spent four or five hours with him. Within an hour of meeting him, he told me: "If you give a customer two choices, where Choice #1 is that you'll teach them everything you know for $500 and Choice #2 is you'll do everything for them for $5,000, they'll take Choice #2 every day of the week."

Wow—people would rather give you $5,000 to do everything for them than $500 for you to teach them to do it all by themselves! Now, was he being a little overly dramatic?

Probably, yet the principle remains: **people want other people to do things for them. They will spend premium prices for you to just take the work off their hands and just serve them.** As I mentioned earlier, for years I said, "Selling is serving." I still believe that, but I've replaced that quote with, **"Selling is a performance." It's giving people what they want the most, and dishing it up bigger and better than any of your competitors can.** More choices. More, more, more! How can you give them more of what you know that they want and do it in a way that none of your competitors is doing it?

And, speaking of your competitors: **competition is a great thing.** Get those negative ideas about competition right out of your head. **The trick is to accept your competitors... and then kick their butts.** There's no better quote I've heard on that subject than one of Ray Croc's. Back in the 1960s, when people were copying the McDonald's system right and left and all these new fast food joints were springing up, a reporter ask Ray Croc, "What are you going to do about all these competitors creeping in on your turf, trying to take away this great thing that you've got going?" Croc said, "The competition is no problem. We'll innovate faster than they can copy." I read that quote in John Love's book, *Behind the Golden Arches*, and I just fell in love with the whole idea. **It's all about innovation—how to serve it up in a bigger, bolder and better way than any of your competitors are serving it up.**

Customers crave and respond to innovation, because it makes it easier for them to get someone to do everything for them. It's not *just* laziness, though of course some of it is. Truth is, we Americans are busier than we've ever been before. We still have the same 24 hours in a day that we had in the past; that's not changed, but we do have more to stuff into that time. People used to do all kinds of things themselves that we rarely do now. Changing their oil, for example: I never do that myself anymore. Chris Lakey says he's never done it at all, and wouldn't really even know how to! When the light comes on and dings at him, he takes the car in to get the oil changed. That's how folks do it these days, and why not? They're busy, and it's cheap. Now, I'd imagine that back when people were first offering oil changes, plenty of people laughed at them and said, "Why would anyone ever pay someone to change their oil when you can do it yourself in your garage?" Yet it's commonplace these days. Some people still change their own oil, but not many.

Speaking of Chris Lakey: until recently, he lived out in the country on 13 acres, and he used to have a certain guy come mow his lawn. Now that he lives in a city lot back in town, this same gentleman mows his yard. He charges $30, and for Chris, that's just too good a deal to pass up. Even though Chris likes to think that he could do it himself, it's *easier* just to pay the lawn man. You see that in all kinds of things that people used to do for themselves. That's a positive thing for the economy, because it provides jobs. **More and more, customers in all marketplaces want someone else to do everything for them. That presents a unique challenge for marketers.**

I'm part of a business that does advertising for people via postcards, and we have two different services for people. We have what's called a "self-service option," where you can just order the postcards; we'll print them for you, and you can apply the postage and a mailing label and drop it in the mail yourself. We also offer a full-service option where you pay us to do everything for you, because we know that many people want that. **This sets us apart from our competitors.**

You need to have that kind of option available whenever you can apply it. You want to say to your marketplace, "Hey, if you want to do everything yourself and have more control, you can do this... but if you want to let us take care of everything for you, we'll do it." **You have two different options for them.** You have to sell people things they want, and you have to give them what they're looking for in the area of done-for-you services. Again: **It's all about them, not you.** That's important to remember, because your focus always needs to be on your customers.

You don't *have* **to do everything for them, of course; some people would prefer to do most of it themselves.** Home Depot used to have this slogan: "You can do it. We can help," which made me laugh, because when I heard that on TV, I'd holler back, "But I *can't* do it!" Still, a lot of people like to try, so you should have that option for your customers, too. (And the truth is, most big home improvement stores do have services where they do everything for you.) If you can prove to busy people that it's worth their time to let you do it for them, and that what you're doing is worth the money you're asking for, then they'll often let you. **Provide good value, offer to do everything for them, and you'll find more and more people wanting to do business with you.**

That's because a lot of people just want to focus on a few things and let other people take care of everything else. That's certainly the way I live my life; in fact, it's my basic business philosophy. I try to do what I'm best at and let other people fill the holes. I do that with my personal life, too. My time is too valuable to be out there pulling weeds, trimming trees, or cutting the grass. I've got other important things to do... so I'm not going to sit there and waste my time doing something that some high school kid can do to pick up some extra date money. That's ridiculous!

I think the done-for-you thing is a growing trend... and again, you don't have to like it, because after all, it's all about them, not you. In a perfect world, you could prefer that it was different... but hey, we don't live in a perfect world. We live in a world where we have to cater to what people want, and what they want is somebody else to do it for them. **If you won't, your competitors *will*. Remember that.** So you've got to make sure in all ways that, when given a choice of doing business with you or your competitors, then your best prospects will always choose to do business with you. We've got to also stay very connected to that quote from Ray Kroc, that it's all about innovation.

Everything that you do in your business is an expense, *except* for marketing and innovation. While marketing is all the things you do to attract and re-attract customers, innovation is all the things you do to kick your competitors' butts while giving customers a bigger, better, and bolder offer that makes them want to keep coming back. **It's all the things that you do to stay extra-competitive: not just competitive, but *extra*-competitive, so that you're the competitor that everybody fears.** You're the competitor that nobody wants to compete against. You're the best in the business.

There's a sense of pride that comes from playing the

game at a higher level than other people are playing it. That's part of the joy of business. That's the attitude and spirit that can take you places that none of your competitors will dare to go. That's where all the joy of life is: that extra mile you force yourself to run. Don't just compete, *over*-compete. **Be the competitor who either makes your competitors go green with envy or tremble in fear. The way to accomplish that is to think about your customers first and always.**

CHAPTER THIRTEEN

"Good Marketing Is A Combination Of Fishing And Chess!"

Eric Bechtold

All great fishermen know that the true secret to catching the big ones is:

1. Use the right bait.

2. Think like the fish!

3. <u>Never</u> reveal the hook.

All fishermen for sales and profits should pay attention!!

Good Marketing is a Combination of Fishing and Chess.

The above is a quote from our good friend, Eric J. Bechtold. We call Eric the young King Midas, because everything this guy touches just seems to turn to gold. **He's got a real talent when it comes to making money.** He's highly driven, very intelligent; nothing will stop him. He works very hard. He was an excellent student of entrepreneurial ways when he was younger, and now he's an excellent teacher.

Marketing is an exciting game—the best sport in the world—**and it really is like a mix of fishing and chess.** Anyone can participate in either activity, but they require a high level of finesse and dedication to do well at. I've known people who were fanatical about fishing, and I've spent a little time with them; but I was never obsessed with it the way they were. These guys lived it, breathed it, ate it (sometimes literally!). Part of the thrill is that you never know what you're going to catch. **However—and here's where it relates to marketing—all great fishermen know that the secret to catching the big fish is threefold. One, you have to use the right bait. Two, you have to think like a fish. Three, you never reveal the hook.** All fishermen for sales and profit should pay attention to those factors, because essentially, we're fishing in your marketplace.

You never know what you're going to get, although you're trying to attract a certain type of person, using the right bait (your offer). So how can you attract the very best customer for you, the person who's going to stay with you for years? How do you hook the one who's going to bring other business your way, the one who's going to spend the most money over the longest period of time and do you the most good? We're not just talking about money, you see. Some of our best friends are our best clients. We love spending time with them. They're positive people.

In order to attract those people, you've got to have the right bait. In this sense, the right bait is the combination of products, services and offers that they'll find the most appealing—things that differentiate you from everybody else in the marketplace. Start with a good strong USP, a Unique Selling Position—or as our friend Russ von Hoelscher calls it, a "Unique Selling Proposition." **What are you offering that all those other companies, both your direct and indirect competitors, are** *not* **offering in order to attract that type of person that you're looking for?** To figure that out, you've got to think like they think. You have to get behind their eyeballs, if you will. **Try to put yourself in their place as much as you possibly can.** Spend a lot of time thinking about them, so you can give them what they want the most.

What people want the most, in all markets, is new stuff. **The most successful retailers in nearly every field are those who consistently offer something new.** You always want to give the customer the feeling that when they walk into the store, it's a little different than last time. That's another growing trend: **people are always looking for things that are at least a little bit new, though not so new that they can't recognize the familiarity underneath.** You don't have to like that, but you do have to recognize it as reality, and accept it and embrace it if you want to make the big bucks.

Chances are, you're like this too. I've already pointed out that given all the choices we have these days, consumers are like spoiled children. A spoiled child is usually a brat, and you just can't satisfy them... especially if they're tired of something. They're cranky, and their attention span is very short. They just can't seem to concentrate on anything. That's the way consumers are these days... and again, you don't have to like it, but don't fight it. **If you want to make money, you have to recognize and embrace this factor.**

So, you've got to offer something new, new, new all the time. When you're thinking like a customer, put yourself in a child-like place where you've got a tiny attention span and a lot of people trying to get your attention. Pretend you're spoiled rotten. You've got all the toys in the world, thanks to Mommy and Daddy... and those toys aren't good enough. **You have to have new things!** They may be stupid little things, but you've got to have them.

I've already mentioned to analogy of the customer as dictator, whereas the saying used to be "the customer is king." Well, nowadays I see the customer as almost like a child dictator. You put them in charge of a whole country, and look out! They're mean kids. I don't mean to be negative here; the market is what it is. **People are subjected to so many choices nowadays they're a little finicky, and they can afford to be.** If you don't take good care of them and constantly give them new stuff, they're not going to complain; they're just not going to come back and do business with you.

And then the third thing: never reveal the hook. That means that you have to sell people without them realizing you're selling to them. There are plenty of ways you can do that, and I could do a whole book on that alone. Basically, though, you want to make all your marketing messages as altruistic as you can. It's all about serving *them*. It's about doing good things for them, and the community, too. Now, this new company we're starting is a local business. I haven't been involved in a local business since my first business 25 years ago—but I know that it's all about fitting into the community, and aligning yourself with certain non-profit organizations. We're a pet boutique, so we're strongly affiliated with the local humane society. In fact, a percentage of our pet food sales will go to the humane society. We're going to broadcast that, so that every time one of our customers comes in to buy pet food, they'll know that a portion of that money is going to help the humane society and their no-kill shelter.

So think about Eric's quote: "Good marketing is a combination of fishing and chess." **We're always fishing for the best customers, but it's a game, too.** There are strategies involved. Actually, a great deal of strategic thinking has to go into all this, regarding exactly how you're going to create the right combination of products, services, opportunities and offers for the people you're looking to hook. You need to put together a package that will be so attractive to them that not only will they come and do business with you once, but they'll come again; and of course, all the profits are made the second, third, fourth, thirtieth time. **The goal is to get people coming back for life and *spending* for life, and to have those customers tell other friends and family and hopefully get those people as**

customers for life. There are exceptions, of course, especially if you're dealing with business-to-business products and services, but for the most part, what I've just described to you is the general overall strategy for all businesses.

This is a good allegory not just for marketing but for business in general, because **all business should be about marketing.** Again, marketing is simply attracting customers and repeating business with as many of them as you can for the longest possible period. Often, local business owners don't think of themselves as marketers; they don't even bother to consider that they have to do marketing to bring customers in. Even when they do, they usually turn their marketing over to some account executive at the local newspaper, and they're the ones telling the business owner what ads to run and doing all the marketing "for them." If they keep advertising heavily in the paper and that's it, well, they're probably getting bland, boring advertising like everybody else is doing. That's not to say there's no value in newspaper advertising, **but you've got to know and understand marketing before you run effective ads in the newspaper—or anywhere else.**

All great fishermen know that the true secret to catching the big ones is using the right bait, thinking like a fish, and never revealing the hook. Sometimes you wonder why certain phrases stick with you... and the above is one of them. Here's another. Chris Lakey tells me had a certain friend in high school whom he doesn't remember 99.9% of the conversations he had with. But there's a certain phrase that always pops to mind in association with this guy when Chris hears the fishing/chess analogy. Now, this might come from a movie for all I know, but the guy's statement was this: **"There's a fine line between fishing and standing on the shore looking stupid."**

The point is well-taken when you think about it from a marketing standpoint. If you're standing there trying to market, and you're not doing the right things, you're just standing on the shore looking stupid. It's like fishing without bait; you *look* like you're fishing, but you're probably not going to catch anything... so really, you're just standing on the shore. **If you're not using the right bait, if you're not thinking like the fish, if you're revealing the hook, you're probably not going to catch any fish.** You literally could be standing there for hours on end doing nothing, being utterly unproductive.

One of the most important things here is that you've got to know what you're trying to catch. That's certainly important when you're fishing. What does using the right bait mean? Well, there are many different species of fish even in just a stock pond here in rural Kansas. You can fish in that pond for anything from tiny bluegill to crappie to largemouth bass or catfish. And even in the catfish category there's flathead catfish, channel catfish, blue catfish, and bullhead catfish. Admittedly, all catfish tend to bite on the same bait; but you *can* catch different kinds of fish, and you're very unlikely to catch a bass or bluegill on the stink baits that catfish love.

Size matters as much as composition. Chris used to have a pond back on his old property. His kids would go fishing, and a lot of times they would catch little, tiny fish; and Chris would always tell them, "It's because you're using small bait." By using small bait, you catch small fish. You'll never catch a whale with a minnow, right? **The bait you use depends on what you're after.**

When you're using bigger baits, you catch bigger fish.

To carry that over to marketing, you have to know who your market is in order to choose the right bait. **You have to know *exactly* who you're trying to catch.** With our new pet boutique, one of our challenges is trying to find out who the pet owners are in our community, and trying to find out how to reach those people. What bait can we catch them with? If we use the wrong bait, we'll catch no customers... or we'll catch the wrong ones. If we use the type and size of bait that appeals to bird owners, for example, that would be a mistake—because we don't have anything to offer bird owners. It would do us absolutely no good to run an advertising campaign to catch bird owners as customers, so we want to avoid that bait. We won't even make the mistake of using the word "bird" in our marketing. Instead, we want to use things that reach dog and cat owners. *We know who we're trying to reach.*

In a more general sense, at the very least we need to use the right bait as it relates to people who like animals. If we were to run an ad that said, "Attention, everybody who hates animals!" well, we'd probably catch *some* attention. It wouldn't be positive attention, because we'd attract the kind of people that we don't want to sell to. Our customers are going to be folks who like animals. In fact, we hope they *love* animals, because we're selling items that are more expensive than the ones you buy at Wal-Mart. We're selling high end, premium stuff. We need our pet owners to really, really love their pets, not just like them a little.

If we ran an ad that targeted people who didn't like animals, we would be reaching the wrong marketplace, catching the wrong fish, because we used the wrong bait. It's like Chris's kids using little bitty bait and catching little bitty fish, and then getting upset about it. When you use the wrong bait, you catch the wrong fish. **When you're looking for a specific fish, you've got to use the right bait.**

In marketing, that means you've got to use the right advertising, the right messages, to reach the right customers. You do that by using the second point here: thinking like the fish. You've got to know who your customer is in order to find out what they respond to the best. Knowing your customer is very important, and that's one of the reasons good marketing is like chess. I've spent a lot of time here talking about fishing, but chess is the other side of the coin. **It's all about strategy, and the way you know the right strategy is to think like your customer.**

If you're going to start a business that reaches pet owners, it's useful if you're a pet owner yourself. If you're selling clothing, you probably ought to wear clothes yourself... or at least the type of clothes your target customer wears. **Be an active customer in the marketplace you're trying to reach. Know what kinds of things they're looking for.** Chris Lakey tells me that if he were going to build a business from scratch, it would probably sell things related to politics. That's because he's a politics and news junky. He knows what kinds of things the people in that marketplace will respond to, since he's a participant in that marketplace himself.

Hobbies and other things you're interested in can be the launching point of a business, because you know and think like the customers you're trying to reach. If you don't know the marketplace you're trying to reach, then you have to spend a lot of time playing catch up and getting into that marketplace, finding out who those people are and what they respond to, thinking like them, so you can be in a position to know what kinds of bait they respond to. Do they respond to a worm, or a lure? Do they respond to live fish? What bait do you use? What marketing methods do you use to attract the customer you're trying to reach?

And again, never reveal the hook. It's important in fishing that you don't, although I've heard of people catching fish with an empty silver hook. It's shiny, and sometimes the fish will see it and attack it, but that's not normally the way you do it. You bury the hook in the middle of the bait. If you're using a live worm, you string the worm through the hook so that they don't see it; all they see is a big, juicy worm.

In marketing, we talk about the hook being the thing you do to get them to respond. It's part of the offer. You never want to reveal the man behind the curtain. You want to make them a presentation, like the worm sitting on a hook in the middle of the water. You want them to focus on the worm, not the hook—you want them to focus on the offer you're making, the thing you're doing to make them come into your store or respond to your email offer in the first place.

Going back to this pet business we're getting ready to start: one of our main goals is to build a huge database of customers that we can not only have buying pet food from us on a regular basis, but that we can make special orders to. We want to be able to send invitations to special events, birthday cards, etc. **We feel our ability to make money is directly related to how many customers we can get on a mailing list so we can**

communicate with them on a regular basis. Therefore, we're going to have contests, give away prizes, and do other, similar things to get people to sign up for our mailing list. If we just told them, "Hey, listen. We have a mailing list. We'd like to mail you offers on a regular basis. We'd like you to become a good customer for life, and the way we're going to do that is to have you fill out this form, give us all your personal information, tell us how to contact you, and you'll hear from us often," well, that wouldn't be very effective. Instead, we offer them an incentive, a benefit. They know we're collecting their personal contact information, but we do it as we run a contest. **We do things to make them want to give us that information.** Really, they're signing up to win some dog food, a prize, or get a gift. **The end result is that we build our mailing list. That's part of not revealing the hook.**

So, fishing and chess. Chess is a strategy game where you've got to outthink your opponent in many ways. Strategy is crucial. There are certain things you have to do if you want to do to win the game; you have to think on your feet. **Those necessary strategies include picking the right bait, thinking like a fish, and not revealing the hook; you mix those in such a way that you come up with the best possible strategy to help you win.** In your business, winning means making more money, serving your customers better, and getting them to respond to your offers regularly. **That's how you keep score in business.** So, think like a fisherman, think like a chess master, and you'll be well on your way to making huge profits. Have some fun. Both fishermen and chess players take it all very seriously, but they're doing what they love to do.

CHAPTER FOURTEEN

*Focus on your strengths
and make sure you have
enough reliable people and
systems in place to cover
your weaknesses.*

Focus on Your Strengths

This secret really *is* a secret for a lot of small business owners. They just don't get it, and I don't understand why that is. It's really a simple idea, like everything else we talk about, and yet it has a huge impact on any business... any human endeavor, really. **Here it is in full:** *Focus on your strengths, and make sure you have enough reliable people and systems in place to cover your weaknesses.* Don't worry about *improving* your weaknesses. Focus on your strengths, and then make sure you have reliable people and systems in place to handle everything else.

Too many people try to wear all the hats in their business, as I've mentioned before. We see this problem again and again. They're convinced that they have to work on their weaknesses as well as leverage their strengths... so they spend a lot of time doing things they're not good at. Do they get better at them? Sometimes, to some extent. But even if they do, they're diluting their efforts, and spending their high-dollar time doing piddly little things someone else could do for a lot less. **Instead, they should focus on one or two or three areas where they can get the biggest results.**

One thing that these people just don't get is that almost invariably, you have a compensating weakness for every great strength. My best example of this is the typical entrepreneur:

somebody who's really good at seeing and feeling the overall vision, somebody who loves to take risks, who lives for getting involved in exciting new things, who craves the adventure of new enterprises, who loves to move forward and try to do big things and go in directions that other people think are impossible. **They have a vision and they try to make that vision a reality. That's the classic entrepreneurial mindset... and remember, they don't even see business in the traditional way.** To them it's a game. It's fun. It's an adventure. It's exciting. It's stimulating. It takes a special person to combine all those things with the drive and determination and the willingness to take on all the challenges required to succeed in business. **It requires a tremendous amount of energy and stamina—physically, mentally, emotionally, and spiritually—to accomplish that.**

But what makes someone a great entrepreneur usually makes them a really bad manager. The qualities needed for somebody to manage a company and to supervise other people and to take care of all of the day-to-day implementation that has to go into making the business run like a well-oiled machine... well, those qualities are usually the opposite of the qualities that it takes to be an effective entrepreneur. **That's why a lot of the companies started by entrepreneurial people just blow up.** Entrepreneurs are control freaks. They want to control every little aspect of the business, but no one can really do that. You've got to delegate most tasks to other people—and I don't mean just *abdicate* them. Abdication is where you just hand something off to someone else and ignore it forever after. **Delegation is where you work through other people.** In fact, I believe that's the smartest work anybody can do: working through the hands and hearts of other dedicated people who are equally as committed as you to making it happen.

It's a smaller way to work, too. It's a great use of leverage. It's a synergy of different people coming together with different qualities, to produce a sum greater than the parts. They all work together, like antique clockwork. Those old clocks are full of gears and wheels and drives. Some of the gears are big; some are quite small. Yet if you take just one of them out, the whole thing stops working. A business is like that. The bigger the business is or the more you have going on, the more gears you have. Those gears represent people and systems.

You should strive to recognize your strengths and weaknesses, so you know what you need help on. We have an associate who is very good at seeing potential problems that other people can't, and that's a special skill. Unfortunately, most people like that are good at finding flaws rather than coming up with solutions. **There's tremendous value in finding flaws, but it takes an entrepreneurial type to find the solutions...** somebody who is optimistic, who can see all of the possibilities, bad and good, and focuses on just those.

But do know what your weaknesses are. Get real about them; don't try to cover them up. **Look for people who are strong in the areas that you're weak in. Systems can help you compensate for your weaknesses,** if only because they let you focus on strengths by putting reliable people in place to cover your weaknesses. For example, **we like to create turnkey systems** for the clients who buy business opportunities from us, whether those systems are for our products or someone else's. **These are all-encompassing systems that handle the entire**

marketing process, from start to finish, for our customer. We provide advertising methods, we process the prospects who come into the system, and we work with them throughout the sales process. That's a complete system, right there.

Lots of people license products; you can find licensed products all over the place. But what are you going to do to sell them? You've got the ability to sell the product, but you've got no system in place to actually attract the customers and make the sale. **So our systems include everything from the item to sell (if it's our own proprietary thing) all the way through the process of actually attracting leads, turning those leads into customers, and then paying out commissions.** That's a good example of a complete marketing system. Similarly, our company has developed systems for managing the entire process of running a business, so you've got that side of things, too. When a prospect comes in the door, we have a procedure in place—even for rudimentary things like opening an envelope, pulling out an order form, taking a check to the bank, or processing a credit card. We have a full administrative system in place. We know where the order originated from, if there's an affiliate we need to pay a commission to, or whether we just need to tag them in the system. **We take this all the way through to shipping, where we identify the item that the person purchased and ship it to them.**

Then there's the customer support. If they call in with questions, we've got people who can speak with them on the phone and answer any questions. Alternately, they can ask for help by mail or through live Internet support. In other words, **we've got a system in place that helps us manage a**

customer's experience from start to finish, so that the customer has the best experience when they're working with us. Those are two different examples of systems we use. They let us focus on our strengths, while covering our weaknesses with skilled personnel who are much better at those tasks than we are.

Let's imagine for a minute that I had a mail order business where I was doing everything on my own—that there was no M.O.R.E., Inc. as we know it. I surely wouldn't be as successful as I am today. I'd probably be working out of my house, not the big building we have at 305 East Main here in Goessel, Kansas. I'd most likely be working out of a spare bedroom, in fact; and when an order came in, I'd have to do it all. I'd have to open the envelope and process the order, running checks to the bank and running credit card numbers through some system. After that I'd run over to my garage, grab a product, box it up, take it down to the post office, pay for postage, and then run back home. And whoa! The phone might be ringing when I got back, because someone who got his package a few days ago is calling. They've got a question, and I might spend 30 minutes on the phone talking to them.

That's what wearing all the hats does. Well, maybe I'm good at one of or two of those things. Maybe I'm really good at boxing and shipping stuff out... but not so good at talking on the phone. But I have to talk on the phone anyway. If that's the case, then my boxing and shipping skills will suffer, because I'm spending so much time talking on the phone. If I were really good at opening envelopes, maybe the talking on the phone and shipping stuff would suffer while I was doing that. If I were good at marketing but not so good at any of those other things, then all those other things would suffer, even though I'm really good at bringing orders in.

Nobody **has everything covered.** There's no perfect person this side of Heaven. Everybody has some things they're good at, and some things they're not so good at. **There's no point in trying to be perfect, so just stop pretending you are and focus on doing the things that you're good at.** Let the other things go to somebody else. **This doesn't mean you should let them go altogether;** you should keep an eye on the other stuff, and help out with it whenever necessary, because it never hurts to hone your skills. **No, it means that you just hire people who are *good* at those things.** Having a system means you're bringing out the best of everybody's abilities. In our case, we have an administrative department made up of people who are really good at doing administrative type things — stuff I'm not very good at. And we have other people who are really good at shipping and being organized, thank goodness.

You want to talk about organizational skills? Our shipping department is huge. All the products have to be accounted for, organized, boxed, shipped—and all that has to be managed on a daily basis. Fortunately, our shipping personnel are really good at organizational stuff and making sure that if someone orders XYZ product, they don't get ABC product. We have people who are really good at that. We have people who are really good and personable to work the phones, too. If you've called us, I hope you agree. Our client service representatives are very personable; they have good people skills, and they're good at that side of things. But maybe if you put one of those guys out in shipping, they would suffer because they're not organizational in that way. **You can see how all of these parts come together to build a system that effectively accomplishes what we need to accomplish in our business.**

If you focus on *your* strengths and then let other people focus on theirs, then everyone comes together (ideally) to make a whole that exceeds the sum of its parts. They come together to create something that's much more effective, and ideally much more reliable, much more organizational, more streamlined, and certainly more profitable for you because of that. If you try to wear all the hats, well... some of the hats, and maybe all of them, are just going to fall off your head. **You can't wear all the hats, so don't try.**

Too often, entrepreneurs suffer from the delusion that they can and must wear all the hats, and so they try to do everything themselves. A lot of our marketing friends are that way. Sometimes they can do it semi-effectively, but I think they're missing out on the benefits of *not* doing it all yourself, and probably costing themselves money in the process because they're trying to do it all. **Instead of being able to do more and more effectively, they do less.** Even if they're managing it adequately, they could be doing a lot more by delegating and by having other people help them with that process.

If you'll do this, you'll be doing what a lot of entrepreneurs just never do. By wanting to control everything, they never achieve as much as they could if they worked through a group of other people. By trying to control everything, they ultimately run the whole thing down. **So you've got to find the very best people you can who have as many different complimentary**

**talents and abilities as possible, and do everything possible
to get everybody moving in the same direction.**

Again, nobody's perfect. We need to stop trying to be
perfect and admit that we're not, admit that we can't do it all.
We have to let other people take up that slack, and here's a
caveat you must keep in mind: **they have to be *reliable* people.
This strategy doesn't say to turn it over to just anybody.**
They must be reliable people that you can count on.

CHAPTER FIFTEEN

❖ ❖ ❖

Blur the lines between your work and play.

❖ ❖ ❖

Blur the Line Between Your Work and Play

The thought is eight simple words: *Blur the lines between your work and play.* **Make your *vocation* your *vacation*.** I think that's one of the smartest business concepts that I've ever run across, and I learned it from a book called *Work is My Play,* which was written by Wallace E. Johnson—one of the founders of Holiday Inn.

One of the things that Wallace says in his book that I like so much is this: **the secret of success is to work half a day.** It doesn't matter which half you work; just make sure you work half a day. Now, you have to take that in its proper context, because he isn't talking about a standard eight-hour workday. **He's talking about a *day*, the full 24 hour period from sunrise to sunrise, which means your "half-day" is 12 hours long!** If that just shuts you down flat, consider this: when you study all the great business successes, you'll see that they were *not* accomplished by people who punched time clocks like most people do. Those people put in their 40 or 50 hours, but their real life exists beyond what they do for a living.

Well, folks, **the secret here is to throw your whole heart and soul into your business.** Just put it all out there. My best analogy for that is the farmer, which is especially apropos here in the Wichita area. Even when you're in the biggest city in the state of Kansas, if you travel just a few miles past the outskirts, you're surrounded by farmlands. Well, farming isn't really a job that people do for money. Farming is a lifestyle. It's a part of who those people are, and it's every cell in their body. It's what they live for; it's their whole identity.

When I think about blurring the line between your work and play, I can't help but think about the standard job mentality. It's all about the money for most of us, isn't it? I've got family members who are like that; my own father was like that. Well, most people just naturally assume that that's what I'm all about, too, because during the past two decades I've been "successful." Hey, it's all about money to them, so it ought to be the same to me, right? Wrong! You know what they say about assuming, right? **For me, it's all about the *game*. It's about the *excitement*. It's about the *freedom*. It's about the fun, the adventure of competing.**

Honestly, that's what business represents to me. I've successfully blurred the line between work and play. **It's all about finding out what you're really good at and running with it, putting your whole passion into the things that you really enjoy and do well.** This morning was a good example: I got up at five o'clock and started working immediately. Noon came rolling around, and I thought, "Wow, seven hours just went by. Seven hours since I got up, and it all just happened so quickly!" I couldn't believe how absolutely fast the time went; it just shocked me. I wondered, *What did I do?* Simple enough: I got absorbed in my work. It became as enjoyable for me as any play. The flow of it all makes me feel alive. It's fun. It's exciting. It's interesting.

I have a little sign on the treadmill where I work out, and it says, **"Do whatever makes you feel totally alive."** That's what a business should be about. It's not just about making money; to me, there's nothing more boring. Whenever you focus on the money alone, or any other single thing, as far as I'm concerned you're going to make the wrong decisions. That's why you focus on the game of it, in its totality, and revel in the excitement, the adventure, of trying to build something substantial. **Try to do something that makes you feel passionate, and just fall in love with your work.** Do what makes you feel most fulfilled, and spend as much of your life as you can in those areas, playing with whatever gives you the greatest sense of joy and fulfillment. **For me it's marketing, it's writing, it's communication.** It's anything that has to do with selling and developing business plans and strategies. **Just don't take it too seriously, or you'll lose track of what really matters.**

Whoever said that business is a serious thing was wrong. Now, does that mean you should laugh at all your problems and just skate by them? Of course not! But at the same time, this whole idea that business is like a prison sentence, where you have to keep your nose to the grindstone and it's wrong to get loose and to relax and have fun... that's an old, worthless idea that you need to set aside right now.

Consider professional athletes, who offer the ideal example of blurring the line between work and play. They get paid to have fun and play games... though, sure, it's a lot of work, too. It's no easy job to be, say, a baseball player who plays 160 games a year from April all the way through September. That doesn't account for all the training and the playoffs, either. They work really, really hard on it; these athletes are very fit, because they stay active and train all the time. *But they're playing.* Even more amazing, they're basically playing a kid's game. Pick-up games of baseball are being played every day across the U.S. and all around the world in their thousands. These guys are doing it for a living... and some are making millions at it. **That's a classic example of getting paid to have fun. Their play is their work, and vice versa. They work hard at it, just like us entrepreneurs. It's about having fun in your business.**

   Now, you can't take this attitude too far, because in order to be successful in business, you've got to take it seriously at some level. That doesn't mean that you have to let it give you a heart attack or a nervous breakdown. Don't take it so seriously that you're exhausted all the time, either. It's okay to be exhausted occasionally, in the same way that a good play session or a good workout exhausts you. In fact, that's a great way to think of it: **it's hard work while you're doing it, but you like the results that come from doing it.** Even if you lose sight of the enjoyment in the heat of the moment, you like seeing what you've gained from it, and you like keeping score. You like going to the scale to see how much weight you've lost or how much muscle tone you're gaining. It's challenging, but it's fun.

   Business should be like that. **Take it seriously and play to win, but remember that it's just a game, and have fun playing.**

CHAPTER SIXTEEN

OPERATION MONEY SUCK:

Invest <u>all</u> of your time, energy, and focus on all the various ways and means of sucking the maximum amount of money from your market.

99% of the focus should be on increasing your sales and profits. This is the life-blood of your business.

No business ever went under for having too many sales and profits!

Operation Money Suck

Operation Money Suck is simple enough. **It involves investing all of your time, energy, and focus on the various means of sucking up the maximum amount of money possible from your market.** I think that a good 99% of your focus should be on increasing your sales and profits, because that's the lifeblood of any business.

With very few exceptions, no business ever failed from making too many sales and having too much profit. **It's *all about* sales and profits;** that's the solution for everything, the one solution that will fix all of your other business problems, as long as you're making those sales and profits ethically and morally. That's where the exceptions come in: businesses have certainly been shut down because they were bringing in a lot of money in ways the government deemed illegal.

Look: you, personally, have to focus on the few things in your business that bring in the largest amount of money. In an earlier section, I discussed how business is like a combination of fishing and chess. So think about chess. There are only six different types of pieces, and that's it: King, Queen, Bishop, Knight, Rook, and Pawn. And yet, with those six different pieces in combination, there are potentially millions of different combinations of moves that you could make. It's the same thing with business and marketing. **There are certain easily-learned**

fundamentals, but there are all kinds of ways to use them, alone or in combination. That's where the finesse comes in.

So spend most of your time thinking about what you're going to do to increase your sales and profits. Really focus in on that, and do it every day. When I'm at my best, I do it seven days a week; though admittedly, I'm not always "On." I try to do something substantial every day to help increase both; just one thing every day. That's some good advice that somebody gave to us many years ago, and I've tried to follow it religiously. Now I'm passing it to you. **Try to do something every single day that could potentially bring you more sales and profit — something that you didn't do the day before, so that you're always moving forward.** Be sure that your head doesn't touch the pillow at night until you've done that one thing. *Focus on your sales and profits.*

I realize that salespeople have gotten a bad rap in some segments of society, and that's one of the saddest things I've ever heard. But you have to get past that. There was a time when I wasn't proud to call myself a salesperson, so instead I'd use the term "marketer" or something similar. But come on: *why* wasn't I proud to call myself a salesperson? Because there's a social stigma against it, caused by a few idiots who give us all a bad name. I'm past all that now, and thank goodness. To me, being a salesperson is something to be proud of. **Salespeople make it happen for everyone else.** It's not that they're more important than everybody else in the company; it's just that the jobs of everybody else in the company depend on the people who bring in the sales and profits in the most direct way. Everybody in the company is responsible for doing their share to keep the whole business afloat—remember, it's like one of those old clocks with lots of different wheels and gears, where each one is important—**but you can't escape the fact that salespeople are the big gears the keep everything else moving right along.**

If it weren't for the people who make it their primary responsibility to bring in more sales and profits, no one else at the company would have a job. It does take teamwork, but I feel that for the average small business, sales and marketing is vitally important—**certainly too important to just delegate or abdicate.** This is that one thing that you should get good at, fall in love with. As I mentioned in the last secret, Number 16, you must blur the line between your work and your play, and a big part of your work/ play should be ways to bring in more money. That's part of the whole fishing and chess metaphor, too: **you have to create systems and strategies to bring in more revenue, so fall in love with all those aspects of the business, and don't just hand them off somebody else.** Try to get good at them; try to learn as much as you can about them.

In the past, I've written several books on the concept of Ruthless Marketing. If you've never read any of them, let me point out that the idea behind Ruthless Marketing isn't quite what you might think at first glance. Most people consider "ruthless" to be a negative term; **but the definition of ruthless as we apply it to marketing has more to do with audacious action, with business aggression.** So when we say "Ruthless Marketing," what we're really talking about is being an aggressive marketer, and going after all the business in your marketplace that can and should be yours, even (or especially) at the expense of your competitors.

I think a lot of people get wrapped up (incorrectly) in the idea that there's a limited amount of money in the marketplace. This is a faulty, ill-placed notion that you shouldn't fall for, folks—this idea that we can run out of money as a society. Yes, individual people run out of money; people do have limited budgets. If you've got ten bucks in your pocket, you've got ten bucks in your pocket. You can't spend $11 unless you want to be like the government and borrow it from China, or put it on a credit card (which is basically the same thing). **But as a society? Oh, there's always more money out there to be made, and there are millions (potentially billions) of people to get it from.**

So this idea that there's a limited amount of money is incorrect. When a business person thinks, "Oh, I don't want to be aggressive. I just want my fair share. There's only so much money in the marketplace, after all, and other people need it too," well... they're shooting themselves in the foot. **First of all, it's not your place to decide to help your competitors; they're your rivals! Second, the marketplace can expand.** Take our new pet boutique, for example. Newton, Kansas has 17,000 people, but I'm convinced that we can expand our reach beyond our city; if we want to and need to, we can expand to *other* cities. We can also get people to spend more money on their pets than they're spending right now. One top of all that, we can also get more people to think about having pets. We're working with the local humane societies, so we can increase pet ownership in town. If we do that, the marketplace grows. And besides, even though there are other pet stores in town, we think there's room for us to compete and capture a big market.

That's the way it is with all businesses. It's not like there's a finite amount of money in the pockets of your customers; you've got to get that concept out of your mind. **Even if it were true, if you can capture a bigger piece of the pie, the more power to you.** We're talking about ruthless marketing here, the overall study of aggressive marketing.

And then you get to this point here: Operation Money Suck. It sounds ruthless; it sounds aggressive. And it is. It sounds really over the top... and it is, purposely. **The idea is that you should spend all your time, all your energy, focusing on the specific ways that you can suck money out of your marketplace.** It's not about going into your customer's pockets and grabbing their wallets and loose change. **No, it's talking about providing real value to your marketplace, and getting as many of your customers as possible to give you as much of their discretionary income as possible.** *Capiche?*

You do that by focusing on the specific ways you can get them to respond—by creating irresistible offers that get them to come into your store and give you their money. **You do that by providing good value,** so that someone thinks, *The money in my pocket is worth less to me than the benefits I'm going to receive by responding to this offer.* **That's what being aggressive as a marketer is all about.** It involves going out there for as much money as you possibly can—and Operation Money Suck is just one way of accomplishing that goal.

There are only three ways to make more money in a business: **you can get more customers, you can get the**

customers you have to purchase more often, and you can get your customers to spend more per transaction. That's how you suck more money out of your marketplace: by providing value to people, and by getting them to decide that they want to spend more of their disposable income with you. You reach that point by knowing your customers intimately, and by doing all the things that I've been talking about throughout this book.

It goes right back to what I was discussing earlier: focusing on your strengths, and then making sure you have other people in place to handle everything else. **Focus on the marketing; that should be your strength.** If it's not, then you have to learn everything you can about it, and *make* it your strength. Let other people do everything else, while you use this method to maximize the amount of money you can bring out of your marketplace. Let them go to the mailbox and ship things and do all the other tasks that are important but don't directly bring in the money.

In order to make Operation Money Suck work, **you've got to make a commitment every day;** and that commitment isn't just about waiting to see what's going to happen. It's a commitment to going out there and trying to *make* it happen, a commitment to taking a more offensive mindset and consistently trying to generate new ideas. The late Peter Drucker, who was a business genius, said that there are only two things in a business that make you money rather than costing you money: marketing and innovation. I've mentioned this concept before. **Marketing and innovation are closely related, because your customers want new stuff constantly.** Part of the innovation is always looking for newer, better, faster, cheaper, more exciting choices to give to the people you're trying to attract and retain as customers.

The more time you can spend on things that are innovative, that get your customers fired up, that differentiate you completely from all your direct competitors, the more money you're likely to make. You'll do even better if you can steal business from all those indirect competitors that your prospects may also consider spending money on. And again, you want people to always know, in their hearts, that every dollar they spend with you is money they're *happy* to spend with you, because what you're offering in exchange is something that they badly want. **Ideally, you can give it to them in a way that nobody else has ever given it to them.**

None of this is easy. In fact, in today's world it's getting harder than ever to do all this, so let's not pretend. We don't sell "easy." But it *is* challenging and interesting. It can be a great adventure, and it's a very worthy thing if you make it your lifestyle. **It's a lifestyle of purpose and challenge, to compete in today's marketplace, where there's an endless number of ways that people can spend and re-spend their money.** Be prepared to accept that challenge. It can be a lot of fun. It's a magnificent game that you play.

CHAPTER SEVENTEEN

STOP wasting your precious time, money, and energy on deadbeat prospects.

1. Do all you can to attract the very best prospects from all the rest.

2. As a general rule, those who have <u>recently</u> spent the most money or who re-buy from you on a regular basis are your <u>very</u> best prospects.

3. Develop new products and services that are as closely matched as possible to what they already bought from you.

4. Try to move your larger prospect group up the ladder — while spending the majority of your time and money on the smaller group of the highest qualified prospects.

5. Think of your entire base of customers and prospects as a triangle with the smaller group of the best buyers at the small tip on top. Can you see it? Good! Go ahead and draw it out. Then think about this: Your #1 strategy is to do all you can to increase the size and quality of the people at the top.

Get Rid of the Deadbeats

You need to stop wasting your precious time, money, and energy on deadbeat prospects. Get rid of them, and focus on the people who are willing to give you their money.

I've got five different points that I want to make here, just to add strength to that statement. **First of all, you want to be very focused on separating the wheat from the chaff: attracting the very best prospects in the first place.** You're looking for the people who will potentially come back and do business with you as often as possible for the longest possible period of time.

Number two, you've got to prioritize. Here's what prioritizing is all about: as a general rule, those people who have recently spent the most money with you, or who buy from you on a regular basis, are your very best customers or prospects for any new, related offer you want to make. **So you need a way to segment out your better customers from the rest and prioritize them. Not all customers are equal.**

Number three: variations on a theme. Develop new products and services that are as closely matched as possible to what people have already bought from you. Try to find ways to give people more of what they bought from you the first time. I'm speaking metaphorically and conceptually, because again, you want to come up with something different but the same. Now, that idea's enough to just drive some people completely crazy: "You want to come up with something different but the same." I can see some analytical types just scratching their heads, thinking I'm an idiot to say such a thing. Yet really, that's what we're all trying to do, at least in a general sense. **We're trying to come up with things that look different from what we've produced before, but have similarities that the consumer can recognize.**

Point number four is, try to move the larger prospect group up the ladder, while spending the majority of your time and money on the smaller group of the highest qualified prospects. The last point sort of puts a cap on number four: think of your entire customer base, and the prospective buyers in your marketplace, as a triangle. Visualize the smaller group of your very best customers at the very top of that triangle. Everyone else has a place in the rest of the triangle, which widens toward its base. **Your number one strategy is to do all you can to increase the size and quality of the group at the very top of that triangle.** Once you visualize that, and once you have a system for prioritizing and determining who your better customers and prospects are, then your whole job is to develop the methods and strategies that get more of those people up at the very top.

This is always going to be a much smaller, more select group of people than the remainder of your customer base. These people spend more money, they come back and buy from you more often, and they refer all their friends and family to you. They're just a joy to be around. **Those are your best customers, and you're always looking for a way to turn as**

many people as you can into those best customers. You're also trying to clearly identify who, in the larger group of people toward the bottom of the triangle, are good prospective buyers but have never bought from you before.

When you do that, you have to adopt a ruthless mindset, so you're not wasting your time or money on deadbeat prospects. In so doing, you're able to clearly see which people are your very best customers, and who aren't. You can see the commonalities they share, so that you can clearly identify the best prospects. **This allows you to focus and prioritize, so that you continue to give those people more of what you know they want the most of.** That's how to get people to come back and do business with you for years.

So stop wasting your precious time, money, and energy on deadbeat prospects. A deadbeat prospect is, essentially, a tire kicker—somebody who is unlikely to buy from you. Sure, some might; there's always that risk, but they tend to be rare. **Instead of placing your focus there, focus on the smaller number of people who *are* most likely to do business with you,** realizing that you might lose some business in between, while you're trying to sort out your best customers from your not-so-good customers.

In an earlier section, I discussed the fishing analogy: that is, how marketing is like fishing in some ways. Well, a dead fish isn't likely to bite, is it? I suppose you *could* hook into one by accident, if you just snagged it while reeling in your line. But otherwise, they're not going to be proactively seeking you out and trying to bite your hook. Well, folks, a deadbeat customer is just like a dead fish floating in the water. Sure, they're there, but they're not likely to do business with you except by accident. **So you have to find ways to separate out your customers, so you know who your deadbeats are. When you do that, you can avoid them.** Why bother spending a lot of time and money chasing down poor prospects who may occasionally buy from you? They're never going to buy often enough or *for* enough to make you a profit.

Incidentally, we actually maintain what we call a "dead fish file" here at M.O.R.E., Inc. **Whenever a customer doesn't buy from us for a three to five-year period, despite repeated invitation, we finally kick them off the mailing list.** To stretch the metaphor a bit, you can't eat a dead fish.

Now, if you had a list of a thousand deadbeat customers and sent them an offer, some of them *might* respond. Let's say five people responded positively. So yes, you made five sales— but what if you needed 15 of those people to buy just to make a profit? You sold to five, so what was the point? **You *always* have to weigh the costs of the mailing versus the number of sales you make.** Of course, you also have to take into account exactly what you're trying to do. If you're doing new customer acquisition, you're talking about acquiring new customers at a loss—that is, spending money to buy and invest in future profits through customer acquisition. That's something different. But if your intent is to serve your existing customers and to try to continue to make a profit off of your existing clients, the way you do that is by focusing on the very best prospects.

As a general rule, those who have recently spent the most money or who rebuy from you on a regular basis are your very best prospects. Recency is very important. When we look at the value of someone on a mailing list, we start with how recently the person has bought something. It doesn't do you a lot of good, or maybe it doesn't do you any good at all, if you have a list of millions of people but they haven't bought anything from you in five years. That list is worthless; those people have no relationship with you, so there's no value there. **It would be better to have a list of a thousand people who bought something from you last month than a million that haven't bought anything from you in five years.** Other than maybe trying to rent out that list, or selling that list to other marketers, it has no more value to you.

Therefore, you need to segment your list based on how recently they bought from you. If you've been in business for five or ten years, don't look at *all* your customers as being on your preferred customer list. They might be on your general customer list; you might mail something to them occasionally to try to get them to come back into the store, but they're not going to be your bust customers.

Consider building a preferred customer list of people who have been in the store within the last three months. How many of *those* customers do you have? Those are your better customers, except for the few who just stopped by for a one-time purchase. **Or go back a year and take the last year's worth of customers, and segment out the people who have been in the store at least four times in the last year.** That way, you can start to build a list by finding people who not only have done business with you recently, but have done business with you on a periodic basis.

Next, try to increase the size of this segment; try to move

your larger prospect group up the ladder, while still spending the majority of your time and money on the smaller group of the highest qualified prospects. **This is a perpetual game in your business of trying to build your preferred customer list as large as possible.** Think of it as a ladder, if you will: at the very top of your ladder you've got all of your preferred customers. Then you've got your regular customers in the middle, and your deadbeat customers are hanging onto one of the rungs on the ladder. **You're constantly trying to get people to move up to another level on the ladder by making them the right offers.**

But at the same time, you're making *special* offers available to your preferred customer list, the people who've already climbed up to the very top of the ladder. **You're serving those people by giving them super-special deals and treating them like royalty. You're trying to keep them on that list, because over time people drop off that list.** There are all sorts of reasons for this, but basically, if you've got someone at the top of the ladder and, for whatever reason, they haven't bought from you in a year, then you probably need to knock them down a bit. They're a less preferred customer now, because they're not buying from you on a regular basis anymore. **You've got to constantly monitor that list and adjust as you go.**

You don't *want* them to drop down, though, so you're constantly making offers to your best customers to keep them at the top, to keep them in your preferred list, to continue to build that relationship that you already have with them. **There's a reason they're on your preferred customer list, and you want to do everything you can to keep them there, to keep them loyal to your brand or your store, and do more and more**

business with them. They like you; they trust you the most. That's why they're there in the first place.

And at the same time, though, you've got to keep trying to get more people to move up that ladder by making special offers to them as well. **Occasionally, say once a quarter, you might want to make them a 'why haven't we heard from you in a while' offer.** Say something like, *This is the last chance to receive our catalog.* You sometimes see catalog mailers tell you they can't afford to keep mailing you a catalog unless you buy something from them. Sometimes they're lying; sometimes they mean it.

You need to mean it. So send them an offer every once in a while that says "Hey, we'd love to keep sending you our newsletter. We'd love to keep you on our preferred client list, but we've noticed you haven't been in the store since the Ice Age. Unless you come in some time soon, we're going to have to say goodbye, and stop mailing you our newsletter or catalog, or sending you special coupons and offers, etc."

Some people will be hanging out in the middle of your ladder. They're not your best customers, but they're not deadbeats either; and that being the case, you need to make them offers to try to get them more involved, to get them to purchase things more frequently. **You're constantly in a state of moving the people on the ladder, you see.** Hopefully people will stay at the top or move up, although people do backtrack or fall down the ladder. Sometimes they move out of the area or the marketplace and fall off completely. For whatever reasons, their lifestyle changes, and they don't spend as much money with you as they used to. **That's one reason you're constantly**

monitoring the numbers and adjusting where people sit on your hypothetical ladder.

I do think that the concept of the pyramid, or triangle, works best here, even better than a ladder. Your smaller group is your best customers there at the top of the triangle; and then the less-special people make up the rest of the triangle, until you're resting on the broad base of deadbeats, or just general customers who don't come in very often. They don't have a really good relationship with you; they might have just bought something from you once. Now, there's not much room up at the tip of the triangle, but it never hurts to do everything you can to increase the size and quality of the group of people at the top.

And I want to you to think about this, too: it's possible to flip that triangle upside down, so that you risk having too many people be your best customers. You might end up with thousands of really, really good customers and a tiny number of average ones. That's what you want, but it's never going to stay that way, is it? You can't defy gravity for long. What usually happens in a situation like this is that you've worked so hard to get everybody on your preferred customer list that the list isn't quality anymore. **That's a terrible mistake, because succeeding in business isn't just about having numbers: it's about having *good* numbers.** It's not just about having the biggest list of good customers as possible; it's about there being a *reason* why those people are on that list.

One thing that you often see, sadly, is companies trying to lower the bar so that they can consider more of their customers good customers. Well, of course we all want the biggest possible number of really good customers, but you end up flipping that triangle upside down if you're not careful. You end up having a preferred customer list which isn't as responsive as it used to be, because you've got a bunch of people on there who don't *deserve* to be on that list. **You have to make them earn that position!** Maybe their qualifier is that they've had to have come in the store at least six times in the last 12 months. And maybe they've had to have spent, let's say, at least $2.000 with you. **So you've set the bar high.** Well, you can say, "Eh, I want my preferred customer list to be even bigger, so I'm going to make it where someone has to have been in the store just twice in the last year. And you know what? You don't have to have spent $2,000. You could have just spent over $500."

What happens? Instantly, that triangle becomes a completely different animal. You've got a lot more customers whom you consider preferred customers. Maybe instead of having 500 preferred customers, you've got 5,000. **And because you made it so easy to get on the list, that list becomes less responsive and, therefore, less profitable.** You've just shot yourself in the foot, because the people on that list have less affinity for you.

So while the goal is ultimately to build that pyramid as big as possible and to have as many customers as possible at the top of it, **you do have to maintain the proper proportions. You always want the biggest side of the triangle to be the bottom, representing the general customer base.** The way to build a larger set of preferred customers is to build the whole pyramid bigger, to allow more people to flood in. Some of those people are going to be average customers; that's fine, because that's the way it is. **You have to work hard to build** up your relationship with that average customer, because that's where your pool of preferred customers is going to come from.

So build the triangle bigger, but don't flip the triangle upside down, or you'll end up in a negative situation where you've got a lot of unresponsive "preferred" customers.

CHAPTER EIGHTEEN

∽MOST∽ self-employed people have a terrible boss!

Most Self-Employed People Have a Terrible Boss!

Most self-employed people have a terrible boss. **That statement sound a little cute, but it's also *true*.** They say that if you get into legal trouble, the worst thing you can do is try to represent yourself in a court of law; you would be your own worst lawyer. It's the same thing with business.

A friend of mine isn't committed enough to really succeed. He's been self-employed for a good number of years now. He has a business, but he's interested in so many different things, and there are so many chances for him to screw around and do everything *except* anything that has to do with his business. **That's one of the reasons why he's always struggled financially: there are so many distractions.** Now, no boss would ever let anybody screw around the way a lot of entrepreneurs allow themselves to. **So just as you wouldn't want to be your own lawyer, you really don't want to be your own boss. On the other hand, it's unavoidable as an entrepreneur!**

Here are a few ways to overcome that problem. First of all, you have to know your strengths and be honest about your weaknesses. I've talked about this before. **You can't fail to take your weaknesses into account;** you've got to take a long, hard look at the things you're not good at, be honest about them, and then delegate them to others who can do them better. **Build a**

team; find other people who are strong in the areas you're weak in. A company is a combination of different people working together. **You've got to build that team, and then set your goals very high.** By experimenting with dozens of ideas, you can find those few things that you can mix up a little to achieve your own highest level of productivity. There are all kinds of things you can experiment with.

Here's an example of one of the things I do in order to be very productive. As I write, I'm six days into a lead fulfillment project. I've got one good day left, and I think I can get it done. So I'll have seven days into it, total. Well, during these last six days, I have just worked my butt off. **One of the reasons I've worked my butt off is because the initial lead generation package is on the press and, if not this week, it'll be dropping the first of next week.** I've got to get this fulfillment package done. If there's one thing I can't stand more than any other, it's to have leads growing cold, because you don't have anything to send to them. It just drives me crazy.

This is just an idea, just something we do within our business. But we'll go ahead and throw the lead generation pieces out there, as I've done now on this piece. **And then, because it drives us crazy to have leads sitting around, we'll work harder.** We'll burn the midnight oil. We'll put in lots and lots of concentrated, focused, intense work of the kind that's unimaginable to most people, because we set it up that way to begin with.

These are things that you do consciously. **Experiment; be creative.** This is just one example of what we do within our business, but there are plenty of things that you can do—and

168

you're only going to find them by experimenting with a lot of things. **Find the things that cause you to work at your highest level, things that force you to be your most productive.** By trying dozens of different things, you'll find a handful that work very well for you. You'll end up working, in some ways, like my example, where we throw these lead generation pieces out there before we have the actual fulfillment materials complete.

It's a way of boxing ourselves in a corner and committing. It's a leap of faith. It's a real commitment. **What you're doing is creating a problem, and then solving that problem.** You're saying, "Bring it on; I can handle that." Without having any real idea about exactly how we're going to put these things together, we make lots of promises to our customers, knowing *vaguely* how we're going to put it all together, knowing that we *can* put it all together... and then we just scramble like hell to figure it out.

What we do then is force ourselves to do what every good boss wants you to do, which is to work your fanny off. Is there any boss who *doesn't* want you to work as hard as you can? When you're your own boss, you've got to do things that keep the blinders on, so to speak, and **give yourself a little taste of the whip every now and then to get yourself moving, to help you stay focused.**

Now, I'll also say that there is power in leverage, and as a leverage principle, a lot of entrepreneurs are actually just high–paid employees themselves. What they should be doing is working *on* the business, rather than working in it. That means different things to different businesses, of course; but essentially, **working on the business is where you're tightly focused on**

the two areas of the business that actually produce a profit, which are marketing and innovation. Marketing, again, is the acquisition and retention of customers; innovation is all those things that make people in the market salivate and want to keep coming back and doing more business with you. If you're totally focused on those areas of the business, then you're working at a higher level than someone who stuffs envelopes. Anybody can do low-level minimum wage work; you don't want to waste your time doing that.

The point is, you want to handle the things that require a higher degree of skill, ability, and talent, rather than just doing the necessary work. It's good, valuable work, but it's the kind of work that almost anybody can do. **As the entrepreneur and business owner, you want to focus on things that only you can do, and that you can do best.** Last, but not least, you don't want to burn out. **So you've got to pace yourself; but you also have to *push* yourself, and learn how to be the most productive worker you can be.**

This whole concept involves realizing, in a visceral way, that as a self-employed individual, you're not the best possible boss. There are a lot of people who really just need to work for other people. Those who are poor time managers, who aren't good self-starters, or who can't manage themselves well in general *need* to work for somebody else, because they need someone to tell them when to work and when to take a break, and when to go home. They don't do very good at keeping themselves busy, doing the things in their businesses that need to be done. If you're like that, and your boss can't keep you in line, then they're not doing a good job as a boss. It's even worse when you're self-employed, so that *you* are the boss.

If you're deep in the trenches in your business, and you have problems keeping yourself in line, then you absolutely have to find a way to be a better boss, to manage yourself better than you do already. **Mostly that comes down to self-discipline. The way to get better at something is to become more committed to it.**

Chris Lakey has a bass guitar that he bought because he always thought it would be fun just to play around with. He wasn't sure whether he'd be committed to learning it or not, he tells me, and it turns out that he really doesn't have the time to learn to play it... or at least, he hasn't *taken* the time to learn. **He has just as much time as everybody else does, but he chooses to do different things with it.** So clearly, Chris isn't a very good boss when it comes to teaching himself how to play bass guitar, even though he has one and he's fully capable of learning. A musician is never going to be able to master an instrument unless they're committed to the time it takes to learn the basics and then practice, practice, practice.

For an athlete, it's the same way. **An athlete's performance is never going to improve unless they practice.** They have to be committed to being better at whatever their sport is. If they're a football player, they've got to commit to better conditioning so they can play more. They've got to be faster, stronger. A basketball player has to be committed to trying to make more shots. A lot of basketball players struggle at the free throw line, so clearly, they've got to get better at shooting free throws. These are the things a coach can stay on them about. **But to a large degree, it's up to them to be** responsible for their own actions and to be committed to improving in these areas.

In the same way, entrepreneurs (or any self–employed people) have to become better at pushing themselves. They've got to find ways to do things that make them more productive, so they can get the job done faster and more efficiently. The strategies that you put in place to do that will determine how good you are at being a boss for yourself. **I think being a good self-boss, if you will, is mostly about using willpower and self-discipline to drive you towards the ends that you're trying to achieve, and setting specific actions in place to become a better manager of your own time and the processes that you employ every day in your attempt to be successful.**

Most self–employed people aren't very good at that, and the ones that succeed the best are the ones who can find a way to pull out the best in themselves. **And you *can* develop the abilities necessary to do that.** As the old saying goes, where there's a will, there's a way. **Your best can continue to get better, as long as you continue pushing forward, keep learning to handle yourself and your time more efficiently, and above all, never stop fighting to overcome all those challenges in your way.**